RIDING OVER HILLS AND VALLEYS

REFLECTIONS FROM A BABY BOOMER

Hi Linda,

I hope you enjoy my little saga! Joyce Elizabeth Trost

RIDING OVER HILLS AND VALLEYS

REFLECTIONS FROM A BABY BOOMER

BY

JOYCE ELIZABETH TROST

www.bookstandpublishing.com

Published by
Bookstand Publishing
Morgan Hill, CA 95037
3267_4

ISBN 978-1-58909-874-9

Printed in the United States of America

Acknowledgments

Not only was the mechanics of writing this memoir a challenging process; it was also an emotional one. Happy times as well as difficult memories took me quite some time to articulate. I owe my indebtedness to my son JT, who showed so much curiosity over our family history, and to my daughter Jen who was delighted with my pursuing this project.

I want to thank my colleague and friend Julie, an English teacher, who encouraged me to begin the process by simply saying, "Just start writing; you'll figure it out!" My friend Jan, a professional photographer, captured a profile picture of me that reflects my interests. Also, a special thanks to my step-daughter Dani who suggested that her friend, Coille, would be a good candidate to be my editor. I could not have done this writing without Coille's patient, meticulous feedback. During the editing process, she would come to know me better than my own family members.

And finally I would like to give a big thank-you to my husband, Dan, who believed that I should treat this arduous task as an enjoyable, retirement hobby with the added benefit of providing a tangible outcome: a book to pass down to younger generations.

Chapter 1

May, 2008

Today is my 59th birthday and I thought I would begin working on one of my goals, which is to write a memoir of my life. I'm actually flying home on a 767 airplane from a wonderful week in northern California visiting my daughter, Jen, and my sister, Cheryl. Such a fabulous birthday present that I had given myself: time with people that I care about as well as enjoying a beautiful area. I promised myself that I would begin writing my story today. So why not begin on my flight home? Without a computer, I'm writing the old-fashioned way, with a pen and some scraps of paper that I found in my purse. However, I'll be transferring my thoughts to the computer to make my words legible as well as using the great invention of spell-check!

It's not that my life is anything exceptional, but this account will give a first-hand perspective into a lifestyle that took place in the second half of the twentieth century, as well as provide some family information that had been shared with me of even earlier times. Writing is not exactly my forte, but I'm doing the best that I can. To be able to pass down my thoughts and experiences to future generations seems like the right thing to do. As I explained to my husband, Dan, "Wouldn't it have been nice for us to be able to read some of the thoughts that our grandparents or great-grandparents had written?" Even now, people are not corresponding with one another through the written word very often, and when we do, it is often in the form of emails or text messaging that can quickly get deleted.

The few family writings that I still possess are from loved ones that have passed away. I have two recipes from my paternal grandmother, Louise: one is on how to make sunshine cake and the other is on preparing spareribs! But I most cherish a few letters from my mother, Betty. In fact, those letters inspired me to write this memoir. I only wish I had more had more of them to better understand my parents' inner thoughts and feelings. There are no writings from my father or grandfathers, since it was the woman's role to do most of the corresponding during those days. So, I'm hoping to share my thoughts, feelings, family secrets, difficult times, happy times, and health issues with the next few generations as well as give a first-hand account of a personal perspective to some major historical events within my life.

My son, JT, has made me a proud grandmother of Romey (age 5). But I am also known as "Grandma Joyce" by my second-husband's five grandchildren: Jack (age 10), Anna (age 8), Joey (age 7), Sarah (age 6) and Maddie (age 6). My daughter, Jen, currently has no children, but she may decide to have children in the future. She actually has eleven frozen embryos waiting for the right time (and maybe the right place) for development. Thank goodness for all the medical advances in recent years which have provided her with the hope of having one or two children.

Jen was diagnosed with breast cancer in 2004 at the age of 32. She had a narrow window of time, between surgery and the beginning of chemotherapy, to extract eggs. Luckily, Ashley, her boyfriend at the time (later became Jen's husband) was willing to provide his DNA to fertilize these eggs. So, maybe one of my descendants may be reading this account and will realize that they were once in cold storage when this memoir was actually being written!

Chapter 2

Early Years: Chicago

I was born in May, 1949 to Elizabeth Mary (Williams) Trost, or Betty, and Vernon Frank Trost. I was one of many in the baby-boom generation, a name given to the surge of a huge group of children born right after World War II. In fact, the births of my two siblings represent the spectrum of ages that are a part of this generation: my brother, Vernon William, was born in June, 1946, and Cheryl Louise, was born in July, 1959. As I was growing up in the 50s and 60s, I enjoyed being part of this evolving, ever-changing group, although some would argue that we were really just a bunch of spoiled brats massive in number.

Our parents had grown up in the Great Depression of the 30s and saw many hardships in life. Mom probably had it the toughest, since she had lost her father at the age of 15, and her mother, a seamstress, was then to be the bread winner of the family. My mother's oldest brother, John, who was in his twenties at the time, gave a portion of his earnings to the family, which definitely helped supplement the household income. There were no governmental programs like Social Security for them in those days.

My father's family was financially better off since his father, Grandpa Trost, had a marketable trade as a brewer, and he could use his skills to provide beer for the immigrant populations in Chicago. Even though the sale of alcohol was illegal during Prohibition from 1920 until

1933, he was able to make a decent living for his family. It seemed that he must have been working in the black market selling beer illegally for a while. The Twenty-First Amendment brought an end to Prohibition in 1933, and brewing beer would no longer be considered a criminal act. I had heard that he actually had made more money during Prohibition, so I'm not sure how thrilled he was to see the amendment passed legalizing the sale of alcohol!

My growing up in the 50s was a fairly innocent time for me. Dad worked Monday through Friday at a company near our home on the South Side of Chicago. Mom was a typical fifties housewife: her life was dedicated to taking care of everyone else in the family. My earliest recollections were of me playing in the front (living) room in our home, which was the first floor of a Chicago-style two-flat. These homes dominated the neighborhoods throughout the city and had the same basic floor plan on each of the two floors: two bedrooms, a front room, dining room, kitchen, one bathroom, and a porch in the back facing the alley.

When I was four years old, Grandpa Trost passed away in the home that he shared with his wife. Later, when I was a little older, I was told that Grandpa Trost had a medical condition, hardening of the arteries, and this affliction caused him to take his own life. It may have been true that he had this condition, but I think there were more serious psychological reasons for his death. I'm sure his suicide was very humiliating and embarrassing to the family, and it was probably easier to explain the cause of his death as being caused from a physical condition rather than a mental one. There was very little awareness about mental health issues in those days. After Grandpa Trost sudden death in 1953, Dad's mom, Grandma, came to live in the flat upstairs. (Since she was the only grandmother that I knew, she has always been known to me simply as "Grandma".)

During the first couple years of my life there was no television set in our home. The technology had been developed, but it was considered a luxury item. Perhaps to bring some joy to Grandma's life, Dad felt that she should be the first member of the family to own a television in the early 50s. So he and his brother, Elmer, purchased a set for Grandma. According to one of my older cousins, this act of kindness created quite a stir with the rest of the two families who did not possess the latest status symbol. Why should Grandma be the only one with a television set? So, shortly thereafter, we also became the proud owners of a TV and life would never be quite the same.

These early sets had a mahogany wood finish and a screen of about eight inches across. And, in the early fifties, everything was seen in black and white only. A couple of my favorite shows in those early years were Ding Dong School and The Howdy Doody Show. There were only a handful of available stations and most shows were done as live broadcasts without filming or taping. To get reception, an antenna was needed and the quality of these broadcasts was not great; in fact they were rather fuzzy indeed. One had to fool with the knobs quite often to get a decent picture. It was not unusual for the TV to "go on the blink" right in the middle of a show due to the many bulbs in the back of the set that could easily burn out. We were so disappointed whenever the TV would malfunction and switch to a blank screen. And it always seemed to happen at the most inopportune time: right in the middle of an exciting program! And with no other options, we would be back to entertaining ourselves, which was definitely not as much fun as watching the latest technology, the boob tube. It would take some time for us to see our favorite programs again since a repairman was needed to come to the house and fix the set. An average household was fortunate to have one television set, and a family would often watch the same show all together in the living room, usually for just a couple of hours in the evening. Of course, there were arguments among family members over which program to watch. As children, we learned that we did not always get our way, and there was no extra TV in a bedroom or family room for us to retreat and watch an alternate program. There were also no remotes to constantly switch stations; we watched one show at a time as a family and most, if not all, programs were suitable for all ages.

In regards to other conveniences in this modern era, a dishwasher was only found in the newest of homes. We had a washing machine with a wringer on the top, but we did not have a dryer. Mom would hang laundry outside on a clothesline in the backyard to dry, but in the winter she would have to use the clotheslines that were strung back and forth in the basement. And most clothes needed ironing, so an ironing board was used constantly. I was taught how to iron as a young girl by using Dad's handkerchiefs. If a mistake would happen on one of these items, it would not be such a huge loss. And believe me, mistakes did happen! Besides my ruining a few hankies, I did also manage to burn the inside of my arm. I had a dark brown oval spot that took years to disappear. Obviously, I never was particularly good at the domestic skill of ironing, and in later life, that inability was just fine with me.

Another sign of the times was that our home had only one telephone, a black, clunky model with a dial. We also shared our phone line with another family; it was called a "party line." When initiating a call, we had to listen first to see if the other party was using the line and, if so, we were to quietly hang up and wait until later to use the phone. But we were always aware that our conversation could be shared by someone else, so we were careful as to what we were saying. Since each phone call was rather expensive, limited use of the phone was expected. It was mostly meant for basic, quick communications or emergencies and not for lengthy conversations. In fact, my brain was programmed at an early age that the ring of the phone could mean trouble, which certainly did not help me later in life, especially when raising teenagers. Needless to say, some of the everyday communication devices that we now take for granted did not exist. There were no answering machines, no voice mail, no call waiting, no caller ID and definitely no cell phones.

Some of the sadder memories of my early life are the issues concerning the polio epidemic. This disease, caused by a virus, was spreading wildly in the early 50s. Since I was so young, I didn't comprehend the seriousness of the illness, but I did know that the disease could cause one to lose the ability to walk, and that seemed very scary to me. The Salk vaccine, which was the first vaccine developed to combat Polio, was announced to the public in 1955. I'm not sure when I actually received my first inoculation, but I'm sure it was a huge relief to Mom and Dad when it was available to us. Our next-door neighbor, Mr. Quoss, who was my best-friend's father, came down with the disease. I believe he was hospitalized and recovered without serious effects later in life. He was one of the lucky ones! Our paperboy also contracted the disease, and I'm not sure how he had fared later on. In 1962, the Sabin vaccine was licensed, which was an even more effective vaccine and could be taken orally. Great, no more shots; just a sugar cube was given to us! I remember huge lines of people waiting at the local high school when this vaccine was being distributed. Years later, polio was almost eradicated from the world, but eventually resurfaced due to the lack of people getting their vaccinations. These two vaccines were perceived as monumental advances in medicine at the time. Many more vaccines would become available to us and our children later on, especially those for childhood illnesses like measles, mumps, and chicken pox. It seemed as if modern medicine was truly protecting us from diseases that could later lead to serious complications in our lives!

One of my favorite memories happened when I was around the age of four or five. I was playing outside in our little front yard when I thought I saw the outline of a man walking a pony. As he got closer and closer, I knew that my eyes were not deceiving me. How exciting! A pony was coming down the sidewalk! I ran in the house jumping with joy. Mom came out and agreed to let me go for a little ride on the pony. The man was actually a photographer and this routine was a gimmick to sell photographs, which totally worked on us. I still cherish the picture of me on that pony wearing my brother's hand-me-down White Sox jacket. I absolutely loved horses! A few years later, I would watch westerns on TV. I wanted to be like the cowgirl Annie Oakley, who was the star of the show. I dreamed of having a horse and being able to be the heroine just like Annie. This show was one of the few that portrayed a woman in an important role. My mother seemed happy as a housewife, but I knew that I wanted more out of life, even at a young age.

Another happy memory when I was five years old was when our brand new upright piano was being delivered to our house. I was sitting on the cement ledge of the front porch when it arrived. How exciting! My brother, Vern, who was eight at the time, began taking piano lessons right away and was fairly talented. But I was extremely envious of him and began being quite a pest around the house about changing my parents' minds over the idea of my taking lessons too. The piano teacher recommended that I wait until I was a little older, but I kept begging and begging. Finally, my parents agreed and I would take my lesson right after Vern finished his. But, after the initial thrill was over, I regretted the amount of time that was required to please my music teacher. I was expected to practice at least one-half hour a day instead of being able to play outside. I began to resent the piano and wished I hadn't been so persuasive. My parents made me continue lessons for the next six years, since I was the one who had promised that I would be disciplined and learn this instrument. It's obvious what the moral of this part of the story is: BE CAREFUL WHAT YOU WISH FOR, IT MAY COME TRUE!!!!

Chapter 3

Dad's Side: The Trosts

My grandfather, Fred Trost, was born in Chicago in 1878 shortly after his family had emigrated from Germany to America. Fred was from the Bavarian Alps where the Trost men were known as the "Tall Men." Each of them was over six feet tall, which was considered quite tall in those days. The word "trost" literally means "consolation" or "trust." My grandmother, Louise Dreher, was born in 1883 in Croosle, Germany, a town on the eastern side of the country. As a child, she immigrated to America in the late 1800s. Both families networked with German relatives in Chicago to get established in this new country.

Fred, in his late twenties, married Louise who was five years his junior in Chicago in the early 1900s and all the extended relatives were happy for the couple. The marriage was fairly typical of the era: the husband was the main bread winner and the wife would be primarily responsible for rearing the children. In 1908, their first child was born, a beautiful girl named Edna, with all the German features of a light complexion with blond hair and big, blue eyes. Grandma must have been totally thrilled to have a daughter with whom she could share so many of her domestic talents. Within a couple of years, Elmer was born with the biggest round, brown eyes and brown hair. They had two more children: Norman, in 1913, and Vernon Frank (Dad) in 1919. Grandma had the perfect beginning of married life in this new country. She would leave hand-written notes on scraps of paper that documented the birth of each child with the date and place. Two were born (including Dad) in the "front house" and the other two were born in the "rear cottage." I assume that there were two houses on the lot where they resided on the South Side of Chicago.

Besides being a wife and mother, Grandma supplemented the family's income by working for rich Jewish families as a cook and housekeeper. She could make the most delicious baked goods: homemade bread, coffeecakes, pies, and other German pastries. She also prepared the traditional German dishes like wiener schnitzel, sauerbraten, chicken and dumplings, and more. Her talents included knitting, croqueting, and needlepoint which were common past-times for women of the early twentieth century. They would decorate dishcloths, tablecloths, pillow cases, and other linens. Grandma was a typical, hard-working woman who came from strong "German stock."

But her contentment with life would soon change and she would never fully recover from the next change of events in her life. As a young child, Edna had gotten very sick with rheumatic fever leaving her with a weakened heart. Eventually, she recovered from the disease, but she remained a sickly child. On October 15, 1921, Edna passed away from complications due to her weakened condition. Although German women were supposed to be tough in times of adversity, Grandma could not rise to that standard. Even later in her life, when she was in her eighties, she would break down and cry if asked about her daughter. I remember one particular time, when Grandma had mentioned that Edna had knit Dad a baby sweater when he was born. When I tried to find out more information about my aunt, Grandma refused to talk about her because it was too painful. So unfortunately I know very little about her short life. In one of Edna's obituaries included this poem:

The window was open,

The curtain was drawn.

An angel flew in –

And our darling daughter Edna was gone.

A previous one from us is gone,

And another message that appeared in another obituary:

Her voice we loved is still:

A place is vacant in our home,

Which can never be filled.

Your Lonely Mamma, Papa, and Brother.

Even though Grandma had the responsibility of raising a two-year old, Vernon, she remained despondent and depressed after losing her most precious daughter. And understandably, she became an overprotective mother in regards to almost any activity in which her youngest son wanted to participate. And then another devastating setback occurred when Dad was ten years old: Norman was killed in a gang-related incident. Grandma, at the age of forty-six, had to go through the nightmare of losing another child. Dad's older brother, Elmer, had been already been on his own by this time and was no longer living with the family. Now, Dad was the only child left on which Grandma could keep her reins pulled so tightly. She was going to do everything possible to protect her young son.

In spite of all of this unnecessary constant attention, Dad matured and grew up to be a tall, handsome young man with blond hair and big blue eyes. He attended an all-boys high school, Tilden Tech, and, although he possessed the physical attributes that would have made in good in sports, Grandma would not allow it, and especially not football. Instead he was allowed to join the cheerleading team. At least through cheerleading, he could be an active, contributing member in his school: this involvement was certainly part of Dad's personality. He did his best trying to please his mother, but I don't think he could ever erase the pain of her losing two children, and particularly parting with her precious daughter. He felt an obligation to give his mother a better life, and Grandma, in turn, would use this behavior to keep control over her youngest son, even as he became an adult. He developed strong convictions to be a good provider for any future family he was to have, but he continued to feel a deep responsibility of being supportive of his mother, both financially as well as emotionally.

Chapter 4

Mom's Side: The Williams

My maternal great-grandparents were named John Young and Helen Mackie. In the mid-1800s, Helen arrived in America from Scotland with a Presbyterian minister but later married John, who was a teamster. The couple had two children, Jane and Sarah (my grandmother). In the early 1900s, Sarah married my grandfather, James Williams, whose parents had emigrated earlier from Wales. Sarah and James would have five children. The first three children, John, Ella, and James (Jimmy) were born within three years of one another. Then after an eleven year gap, Elizabeth, or Mom, was born in 1920 and two years later George came along. I think Mom's birthday is particularly significant because her birth year represents the year that women in our country were guaranteed the right to vote in national elections under the U.S. Constitution. In fact, the law came into effect only five days before Mom was born. How unbelievable to think that my grandmothers could not vote in national elections until they were almost forty years old! I wonder what each of them thought when finally receiving equal recognition under the U.S. Constitution?

My Uncle Jim had told me that he and Ella, during their teen years, would have to rotate babysitting duties for Mom (Betty) and George. Jim wasn't thrilled about this responsibility and would argue with Ella about whose turn it was to be "stuck" at home watching the little ones. Jim loved playing baseball with his friends on the neighborhood streets on the South Side of Chicago and also enjoyed hanging around Comiskey Park, home of the Chicago

White Sox. Mom's brothers were all fans of this South Side team. Sometimes they would earn a little cash by renting cushions, which cost a nickel a piece, for patrons to sit more comfortably in the stands at the park. Mr. Comiskey, the team's owner, knew my uncle and called him by his nickname, Jimmy. Often Mr. Comiskey would open up the gates of the park to the local kids and underprivileged men in the neighborhood and let them watch one of the games free of charge. He was also very sensitive to physically challenged individuals that would arrive at the ballpark in order to pass some time, and he would routinely allow them to enter without paying as well. Even though I became a Cubs fan later in life, the White Sox organization holds a special place in my heart. The park is now called Cellular Field, renamed to provide more revenue to the club. But, I have a hard time thinking of it as an extension of a cell phone company, so I prefer to call it "Sox Park." Mr. Comiskey was not just a businessman but seemed to be a kind individual to ordinary people in his community.

xxxxxxxxxxxxxxxxxxxxxxxxxxxxxxxxx

While in my thirties, I became a golf enthusiast and was able to share my new hobby with Uncle George, my mom's younger brother. Since I've never been an early morning type of person, I'd ask him what time would be the absolute latest we could meet to play golf and he replied, "6:30 am." So we would meet periodically to play at least nine holes and often go out for breakfast afterwards. One of my favorite fondest memories on the links with "Uncle G," was at Arlington Lakes Golf Course when I made a hole-in-one! I hadn't seen the ball actually go in the hole due to the early morning sun that was shining right into my eyes, but as I approached green one of the grounds men said to me, "Do you always play like that?" And Uncle G excitingly said, "Check in the cup!" Since I didn't see my ball on the green, and knew that I had hit it fairly well, I looked down into the cup and there was my ball! I couldn't have been with anyone more special than my uncle to witness such a rare event. That old, cruddy ball is actually still displayed on the bookshelf in my living room. That day was certainly a special one for me to remember with one of my very favorite relatives, Uncle G.

On another occasion after a golf outing with Uncle G, we went for a quick snack and I made the uninformed comment that there wasn't any history of cancer in our family, so we did not have too much to worry about. He had just taken a gulp of coffee and was fighting hard not to spit it back up. He responded with a big smirk on his face, "Have you been smoking dope or what?" He informed me that both of his parents, my grandparents, had died from the big "C." I had had no idea since Mom had always been very secretive about family issues and had never shared that family history with me.

My grandfather, James Williams, died from colon cancer at the age of sixty-three. When I was young and had asked Mom about how Grandpa Williams had died, she had replied from bowel obstruction, which meant absolutely nothing to me. And technically, she was correct even though it was caused by malignant tumors. He had been ill for some time before his death and was unable to work and support the family. The family had had a few rough years, and big brother, John, would help the family make ends meet financially, since there were no government programs to give aid in those days. They were a close, loving family even though they struggled financially. When my Uncle Jim got married to Doris Wesley on August 10, 1935, they decided to have the ceremony at the Williams' home so that my grandfather could witness the event. He died the following month when Mom had just turned fifteen years old.

Currently, colonoscopies are suggested to be given beginning at age fifty to make sure small polyps do not show signs of any cancerous cells. I had the "joy" of having the procedure at age fifty-six and two polyps were found. One of them had pre-cancerous cells from an inherited type of cancer called adema. I'm now on a three-year plan to check for more polyps, and I'm thankful that I have the information to be proactive against a horrible disease. In fact because of my inheriting the colon cancer gene, all family members are suppose to be screened for colon cancer starting at the age of forty. I'm so glad I had that conversation with Uncle George!

When Uncle George shared the information with me that both grandparents were victims of cancer, I asked him for more information concerning my grandmother's death. He responded with his typical brand of humor: "They opened her up, and they closed her up." Her body was full of cancerous growths which could have begun anywhere in her body. She lived to be sixty years old. I used to think that was a pretty ripe, old age, but with my sixtieth birthday looming soon, it doesn't seem so ancient anymore. For the record, there were a few more medical concerns in the family. Aunt Ella, Mom's sister, had a melanoma type of mole removed from her lip, but luckily, had no adverse reactions later. She also had suffered from glaucoma which caused her vision to be impaired. (At the age of sixty, I was diagnosed with an early, mild form of this genetic disease which is totally controlled by medication.) Uncle John died from complications of bladder cancer at age seventy-nine and his son, Wayne, my dear cousin, died of larynx cancer at the age of only forty-eight. No wonder Uncle George thought I was nuts in my statement that there was no cancer concerns in our family!

One more interesting fact about Grandma Williams is that she enjoyed placing twenty-five-cent bets on "the ponies," or horseracing. She would place these wagers with the bookie at the local drug store; maybe her Scottish ancestry had some influence on her by pursuing this pastime. But since the family struggled financially, I rather doubt that she was very successful at gambling, or whether she actually had the opportunity to make many lucrative bets. Since entertainment was so limited in those days, it must have given her a little excitement with the added possibility of making some extra cash.

By the age of twenty-one, Mom had lost both parents and was basically on her own. Luckily, she was very close to her sister and brothers as well as her best friend, Dorothy; all of whom gave her much needed support. At this time in history, World War II was being waged in Europe and everyone in America was getting nervous over the possibility of the U.S. joining our allies in Europe. Dorothy was dating a young man named Norbert and he had a handsome cousin, Vernon, so she introduced Mom to Dad. And then in 1941, the Japanese bombed Pearl Harbor and our country officially entered the war. Dorothy married Norbert and he left home to join the navy. Dad wanted to hold off on getting married until the war was over. He began the process of enlisting in military service because he wanted to serve his country like so many other young men of his age. He even attended his own going-away party that someone had thrown for him. One of the photographs of him at his party showed a smiling, happy man with the American flag hanging in the background. However, he had to share his plan with his ever-controlling mother, who had a major meltdown over the possibility of losing her youngest son in a war with Germany! Dad's manufacturing job was considered important for the war effort, so he was able to satisfy his mother's fears and avoid military service by continuing to work at his company instead of serving his country. He stayed back in the states while almost everyone that he knew in his age group was sent overseas. I'm sure he was embarrassed and frustrated over the whole situation.

By 1945, Germany had surrendered to the Allies, and we finalized the end of World War II by dropping two atomic bombs on Japan. There were all sorts of parades celebrating the American soldiers coming home. For many years to come, World War II would simply be referred to as "The War." It was totally understood which war everyone was always talking about. Even during my childhood in the 50s, old war stories were constantly discussed at parties and family get-togethers. And, on those occasions, Dad would have to remain silent. He had desperately wanted to serve his country, but couldn't manage to hurt his overly cautious mother. I can understand that she could not deal with the possible loss of another child, but her fear, in my opinion, contributed to the erosion of his lack of self-esteem that would haunt my father years later.

In August 1945, since The War was over, Mom and Dad felt it was the right time to get married. And within a year, my brother was born the following June. I was born three years later and they continued saving money to plan for a more comfortable life together. Dad attended evening classes part time at Illinois Institute of Technology for several years while he began his career as an industrial engineer. Later he was promoted to several management positions, but he always regretted not completing his college degree. Dad loved working hard to support his family and was climbing up the corporate ladder without that coveted degree. Mom was content to be a 50s housewife married to a successful businessman, but her marriage vows would periodically be tested by having to deal with a demanding mother-in-law. Mom never complained to me, but I witnessed how self-absorbed my grandmother could be, especially as I became older. But Mom and Dad had a solid, happy marriage with both parties respecting one another immensely. Dad was the first to correct us kids if we demonstrated any poor attitude toward him or Mom. He would say quite sternly to us, "Who do you think **you** are speaking to?" And he was one hundred percent correct in his disciplinary tone: we needed to be put in our place quite often!

Chapter 5

The Times They Are A-Changing
Bob Dylan

A big milestone in my life would be the planning of the building of our new home in the Western Springs, a suburb of Chicago. Mom made me promise not to tell anyone that we were going to move out of the neighborhood. In those days it was quite common to keep family secrets, of which I had no problem doing. In fact, when it was time to reveal it to my friends, I really wasn't that excited about divulging this well-kept secret. I did eventually tell my best friend, Kathy, and I was surprised at her reaction: she began to cry. Kathy was one year older than me, and perhaps much wiser than my total of seven years on this earth. She must have realized that our friendship would never be the same and she was right. Her family also moved out of the neighborhood within the next couple of years. On one occasion, our families did get together for a picnic, but after that day, we stayed in touch only through Christmas cards and eventually lost touch all together.

It was the mid 50s and Dad was getting very nervous about the "changing neighborhoods" in the city. Chicago had very distinct ethnic and racial areas. When a Negro, which was the proper term for African Americans at that time, moved into an area, the fear in those days was that the homes in that community would lose value. The exiting of Caucasians from the city to the suburbs was called "White Flight." The boundary between the Negro area and us was getting rather close and Dad, the businessman, was worried about losing his biggest investment, his home. I don't think of my father as a racist, but he did grow up in a totally different time when there were many prejudices against not only African Americans, but also other ethnic groups and religious affiliations. In fact, Dad's older brother was killed in some sort of gang fight at the age of sixteen. My belief is that he was aligned with a neighborhood German gang and some altercation occurred with another ethnic group. I was told that he was kicked in the chest, and that incident had caused his death. So Dad as a young child was raised to be leery about people from different races and ethnic groups. I'm not proud of this part of our family background, but it is the truth, and I feel it's not my job to be judgmental. I'm not sure how well Dad even knew people of different races, but my guess is not very well. I really believe his greatest motivation to move from Chicago was to protect his family financially. A most important priority in his life was to be the sole caretaker of his family even though this ideal would eventually prove to be a source of great pain to the rest of us in the family

Chapter 6

"Western" Expansion

It was February 1957 and we were moving into our brand new beautiful split-level suburban home. The neighborhood was called Springdale of Western Springs and initially the development had about six different models from which to choose. The home that Mom and Dad had picked had three bedrooms and two full bathrooms with basic plumbing placed in the basement for an eventual powder room. How great it was going to be not to share one bathroom with the whole family, especially an older brother! Since it was winter when we moved in, the landscaping would be finished later in the spring. There were two large hills of dirt in the backyard in which the neighborhood kids and I could use for exploration and adventures. Playing outside was so much fun in this new environment!

Within a day or two after our move, I met my next best-friend, Susan, who lived two doors down from us. She was one year younger than I was, and she had the same love of horses that I did! We were cowgirls that rode our make-believe horses all over the neighborhood. We each had an old broom that had a rope (a rein) tied toward the top of the broomstick. Our imaginations would bring us to riding our horses in the Wild West and helping someone in distress. Our bikes would also have reins on the handlebars, so we were constantly on "horseback." By loading our dolls onto a red wagon and pulling it with one of our bikes, we could simulate a wagon train adventure, just like on the westerns that dominated the television programs. We would head out to the wilderness, which was the undeveloped land that eventually would become more houses in the subdivision. This style of play lasted for several years; I probably was in junior high before I took the rein off my bike. And in fifth grade, I was given the best gift of all: horseback riding lessons! Mom drove me every Wednesday to Keith Lyons Stable in Oakbrook where I learned how to ride the most elegant horses using the English style of riding. I'll never forget beginning on sweet Sally, an old black and white, but then graduating to my favorite horse, Nifty, who was a chestnut-brown part-thoroughbred. I only took lessons for one year, but I was the happiest fifth grader in the world. Another exciting event was about to happen that year, so the expense and time involved for Mom to drive me to lessons was going to come to an end. I loved being given the opportunity to have one year of living my childhood fantasy and felt no resentment when it was time to let it go.

When we first moved to Springdale, Susan had one younger sister, Linda. But a year or so later, I found out that Susan's mom was having a baby. I was so envious of Susan after she became the proud big sister of a baby girl, Terry, that I let my jealous feelings be known around our home. Even though I had a big brother, it was not the same as having a little sister. I continued to pester my parents about having another baby. I like to think that I actually had something to do with the eventual conception of our new baby, Cheryl, who was born in 1959. Mom had told me years later that she and Dad had planned this pregnancy, even though she felt the neighbors thought that Cheryl's birth was probably an "accident." My brother was thirteen and I was ten, so it seemed unusual to plan a pregnancy with such age spread between siblings, and Mom was almost forty years old as well. But I was so thrilled because

I had another dream come true. Even though my horseback riding lessons would be over, I was now going to become a big sister!

All of our neighbors had children in the Baby Boomer Generation, but Vernon and I were among the oldest in the neighborhood. Summer was an exceptional time for me while I was growing up. We could play outside until dark, which meant that there was time even after dinner to be outside. I hated wasting time to come in to eat, so I'd gobble down my dinner as fast I could so I could and go back outside with my friends. We also spent many hot summer days at our local swimming pool. We did not have central air-conditioning, so the pool gave us instant relief from the oppressive heat and humidity of a Midwest summer.

Towards the end of summer, my brother and I attended East Bay Camp for one week. It was so much fun to sleep in cabins on bunk beds and to enjoy the benefits of being on a lake with swimming and boating available. I became good friends with a girl from Peoria named Cindy. We would request to be in the same cabin with one another every year from then on, and we would write letters to each other throughout the school year. My parents probably really enjoyed a week without my brother and me around too; I'm sure it was a lot more peaceful! But I had mixed emotions about going to camp, since it signified the ending of summer. School would be starting soon and I wasn't at all excited about that routine: in fact, I dreaded the beginning of each new school year. Some of my friends were bored and ready to hit the books again, but I was never in that frame of mind. Looking back at my old report cards, there was a definite pattern in the teacher comments regarding my lack of enthusiasm in beginning of the school term. But those concerns seemed to only be evident during the first quarter of every school year, as the comments improved for the remaining three quarters. It's kind of ironic that later in life, my career choice was for me to be a junior high school science teacher. Even then, I wasn't very thrilled with the start of every school year! However, that uneasy feeling would not last long as I was thankful to have such a dependable career, to earn a livable income, and to have the ability to be an independent woman.

Chapter 7

Fun at Home and on the Road

For the most part, Mom and Dad were very frugal with the family expenses. Home-cooked meals were the norm since going out to a restaurant for dinner was only done on special occasions or on a family vacation. However, as a member of the Shrine organization, Dad would support some of the association's charitable events that usually included dinner and dancing at a nice nightclub. To save money, my parents would usually throw a pre-party first at home inviting other couples for cocktails before leaving for the event. This practice enabled them to enjoy one another's company, as well as loosen up their demeanor for the affair. Luckily, no one seemed to get too looped before driving into the city! There was no such thing as a designated driver in those days!

Within our extended family, our home in Western Springs was usually the epicenter of any special occasion: birthdays, holidays, celebrations, etc. Sometimes a little too much alcohol consumption would take place, and occasionally, the next morning there could be an aunt or uncle sleeping in one of our bedrooms. One birthday party for Grandma, probably her 80th, Uncle George, being a little silly and a bit too hammered, poured a drink over someone else's head. Most everyone thought it was funny, except for his wife, Aunt Helen, who left the party early without Uncle George. I'm sure he was in the doghouse for quite awhile after that episode!

As a kid, I thought these family parties were so much fun! And in the morning I would sample some of the leftover cocktails. Luckily, Mom did not clean everything that evening, but would wait until the morning. My favorite was the popular drink, known as a "high ball," which was made with bourbon and ginger ale. Yum! I did not care for Scotch whiskey, which was another favorite of my older relatives: I thought it tasted like medicine. Beer was available too, but wine was not served or ever requested. It simply was not a mainstream beverage at that time. My parents allowed me to sample small amounts of alcoholic beverages at family gatherings. I'm sure they thought that it would be safer for me to experiment in front of them instead of sneaking some drinks with friends when they weren't at home. Neither Mom nor Dad drank much alcohol on a regular basis: it had to be a special occasion. Dad, who was slightly overweight, did not want to waste the calories on a beer. I remember him commenting that he would much prefer a milkshake over a glass of beer. In fact, ice cream was his favorite dessert, and it didn't have to be anything fancy: plain vanilla ice cream was just fine.

With few exceptions, my family usually went on a nice, annual summer vacation. Mom and Dad saved all year so we could drive somewhere interesting, and we'd become typical tourists trying to seek out all the sights in the new area. Dad enjoyed being the driver, and traveling long distances were not uncommon. One of the most interesting trips was an eight-thousand-mile adventure in July of 1960 when the five of us piled into our Rambler station wagon and headed out west. Cheryl had just turned one, I was eleven, and Vern was fourteen. We had no air-conditioning, no seat belts, and no child seat for Cheryl. So luckily, I could crawl into the back of the car along with the luggage when I got restless and needed to stretch out. I would play a lot with Cheryl and read the state maps to kill time when traveling all day in the car. Vern was an avid reader so he'd have his nose in a book for most of the trip. Mom and Dad had to carefully plan the finances involved with the trip since the use of credit cards was nonexistent; only cash or checks were used. We would often eat breakfast and lunch from the goodies, such as Spam that was in our cooler, and then we'd have a nice dinner every night in a restaurant. I usually ordered the second cheapest item on the menu, and Vern almost always ordered a hamburger, which probably was the cheapest item available. He wasn't trying to be frugal: he was just being a teenage boy without an adventurous palate. We would usually find a motel with a swimming pool, which was a huge treat for us after being cooped up so long in the car. On traveling days, we would be on the road by 5:00 a.m., so dad could make "good time" before looking for another motel room later that afternoon at our next location.

The first leg of this monumental trip included visiting the Badlands, Mount Rushmore, Glacier National Park, Yellowstone and ending in Seattle, Washington. Dad held a position of some authority in his company, Continental Can Company, and this decision-making power enabled him to plan business meetings at various times and places. So, he conveniently planned a meeting at the plant located in Seattle during the first week of July. We stayed in a cabin just outside the city for a few days while Dad commuted into town to do a little bit of work. That was just fine with me to take a break from the long periods of driving in our Rambler station wagon. Dad also was trying to stretch out his vacation days the best that he could. Our family visited nearby Mt. Rainer and played in the snow near the top of the mountain. This little adventure was the only time on the entire eight-thousand-mile trip that baby

Cheryl was upset and cried in the car. She was probably in pain from changing altitudes and her ears must have been killing her. But after we got back to the cabin there wasn't another whimper out of Cheryl again for the remainder of the vacation. Such a good baby she was indeed!

After leaving Seattle, we headed south on either Highway 1 or 101 which was a beautiful, but long ride through the endless redwood forests of Oregon and Northern California. Eventually we crossed the Golden Gate Bridge and entered San Francisco. We spent a day in the City by the Bay being typical tourists riding the cable cars and visiting Chinatown. Our next stop was Yosemite National Park, and I was so excited because there were no lodge rooms available: only tents with wooden floors. I was finally getting a taste of camping outside like the cowboys did! Mom wasn't so thrilled about having to walk to the bathrooms, but I was in heaven. Even at the age of eleven, I was mesmerized by the beauty of this majestic place. I told myself that I would love to return some day to see the waterfalls and canyons again. Vern and I would hop from one giant boulder to another underneath the main waterfalls. Those areas are now roped off so visitors won't get hurt. Luckily, I've been able to return to my favorite national park several times, and I still feel that Yosemite is one of the grandest places I've ever visited!

Chapter 8

Anxious Years

Transitioning to junior high from elementary school was the next big deal in my life. Beginning in September 1960, I entered Highlands Junior High School as a sixth grader. We were now in a separate building, but it was right next to the old one so it really wasn't such a major change. My classmates and I were able to experience six different teachers instead of just one, and we traveled from room to room in the process. Most of my teachers were fairly interesting and even considered quite unique. However, some were not so inspiring and, in fact, rather boring. We now were not "stuck" with the same teacher all day long, and school seemed more fun with new responsibilities. I was also expanding my friendships to girls that did not live in the immediate neighborhood; as a result, Susan and I began to drift apart. After all, I was a whole year older than Susan and that age difference was a big deal in junior high!

Sixth grade is the time when I became interested in boys. There were sock hops after school where we would practice our dancing skills to the beat of our favorite rock-and-roll songs. One of my favorite television shows was American Bandstand, which was broadcast live when I arrived home from school. I'd watch the new dances and try to emulate them. But the boys in sixth grade were not ready for dancing even though they attended the school events. In addition to the occasional sock hop, we were exposed to some formal dance lessons: sixth graders had square dancing, and seventh-and-eighth graders learned social dancing called Fort Nightly. Now the boys had to dance with the girls under adult supervision, which seemed pretty cool. But we preferred our own style of dance at private boy-girl parties, usually taking place in someone's home with the lights being turned down low. Johnny Mathis songs were always popular at parties since these songs were slow and romantic. Our style of dance consisted of us just rocking back and forth with our arms around one another – not very difficult at all. Our hormones were definitely beginning to take off!

If a boy wanted to "go steady" with a girl, he gave her his ring which she wore on a necklace. This fashion statement was called "wearing a ring around your neck" and, if you were lucky enough to receive one, it was considered a form of high status! However, "going steady" did not mean all that much in junior high. Actually, you spent most of your time talking on the phone with your boyfriend and eventually seeking out one another each at parties or dances. Around this time, our generation coined the phrase "making out" which was just a romantic style of kissing. Our parents weren't sure exactly what the term meant and imagined that it was something more risqué than it actually was. And we didn't mind keeping our parents guessing about what we were up to either!

The early 60s was the beginning of the period when the Baby Boomers were becoming a rebellious group. It began with our style of music, rock and roll, which was not like the melodies our parents enjoyed during World War II. There were all sorts of musical artists and groups popping up: The Supremes, Frankie Avalon, Little Richard, Little Anthony and the Imperials, Buddy Holly, Elvis Presley, The Everly Brothers, and many more. AM radio stations played the hits of the sixties and I particularly liked the top ten countdown of songs that were played from 5 p.m. to 6 p.m. on WLS. There were record stores that had listening rooms where you could hear various records, or 45s, before purchasing one for 99 cents. The hit song was on one side of the record and some unknown song was on the back (which was seldom listened to). My allowance, of 50 cents a week was saved along with my babysitting money, and would often be spent on a favorite record. My friends and I would get together and listen to our 45s for hours, and we'd bring them to sock hops and parties too. Brightly lit juke boxes, stacked with 45s, were in most casual restaurants; it usually would cost a quarter to play three songs. These juke boxes became musical icons and symbolized the good times of this period; later they would become valuable collector items.

Besides loving the popular music of the sixties, I was very excited to be chosen as a member of the cheerleading squad. There were no organized sports at school for girls and being a cheerleader was one of the few physical activities offered. I was so proud of myself to have made the 7th grade squad as a 6th grader. Then, the following year, I was told that I had the highest points during tryouts and was named the captain of the 7th grade team. Our sponsor, Mrs. Herrin, was someone everyone really liked: she was young, pretty, and had a southern accent. The last thing I wanted to do was to disappoint her. But at one of our practices, I complained about the 8th graders using one of "our" cheers that was supposed to be just a 7th grade cheer. I'm sure I voiced my complaint in a manner that was not becoming of someone who was supposed to be the leader of the squad. During the next practice, Mrs. Herrin demoted me from being the sole captain to sharing the title of co-captain with two other girls. At first I was embarrassed and upset, but she actually did me a big favor by addressing my poor attitude. The other two girls were very sweet, and it was not a secret that she always had favored them. This new arrangement of sharing the co-caption's responsibility was really better for the entire squad, and it was a wake-up call for me to work on more tactful communications.

The following year, I learned another lesson of humility: I almost did not make the eighth-grade squad. I had just enough points during tryouts to be a substitute and not a regular team member. It was another demotion and I felt very humiliated, but at least I was still able to go to practices, wear the uniform, and cheer in most of the routines. The whole experience helped me mature, which I surely needed. Cheerleading also helped me improve my social skills, but it was too bad that there were not more opportunities for the girls who were not lucky enough to be on the squad. Later, in the 70s, there was a federal law passed called Title IX, that required public schools to provide equal opportunities in sports programs for girls. That eventual change would be a huge improvement for young women and was so greatly needed!

One day in the winter of 1963 after leaving a basketball game, I had become quite hot and sweaty from cheering in the musty gym. I looked around the parking lot for my ride home in the cold winter air, and I left my jacket unzipped since the frosty air felt good. It was rather fashionable in those days to keep one's jacket unzipped. As a result of my "hip" behavior, I developed a deep cough with a lot of congestion in my lungs, and it turned out to be bronchitis. However, when visiting our family doctor, he was much more concerned about my spine than my lungs because my back was showing quite a pronounced curvature. The same doctor had mentioned a year earlier that I had a slight curve, which was very common, and it was nothing to worry about. How wrong he had been! The condition is known as scoliosis and my curve was an "s" shaped one. I had no noticeable pain that time, but my body had become disfigured. The cause of this condition was probably due to genetics, but I wondered if the severity of the curvature had something to do with my poor posture. Another possible theory was that I had contracted polio and never knew it, since the disease could cause scoliosis. I also do not know if the first polio vaccines, which were more potent, could have contributed to the problem. But no matter what had caused this condition, I needed to see an orthopedic surgeon in Chicago every six months. I would have an x-ray with every visit and measurements would be taken to see if the curve was worsening. The periodic examination would make me very nervous because I did not want to have a fairly serious operation. If the degree of my curve were to increase, my backbone would have to be fused together with the recovery time taking a full year. The thought of this having type of surgery was devastating to me. Not only would I be out of commission and away from my friends, but my body would become much less flexible and quite stiff. My doctor felt that once I stopped growing the curve would not worsen and I wouldn't need the constant appointments. Luckily, my condition remained the same throughout high school and I hadn't grown taller since eighth grade, so I stopped seeing the surgeon when I went away to college. Actually, as a person ages with scoliosis, the curve usually worsens over time and can become quite painful. Just because a person stops growing is not a guarantee that the curve will remain stable. In hindsight, I question if we had done the right thing, but I do know that the techniques for back surgery were not very developed at that time, and a whole year for recuperation now seems ridiculous. I also enjoyed having a lot of flexibility with my body and would have probably missed out on some activities that I had enjoyed in high school and college. So my parents and I probably did make the right decision for my health at that time of my life.

Besides worrying about my personal life, I was becoming aware of the political issues beyond my secure suburban environment. The USSR, also known as the Soviet Union, was a powerful conglomeration of communist countries, with Russia being the most influential of all of them. The Soviets were developing different missiles and atomic weapons and there was a lot of fear in our country about how we were going to protect ourselves. Even though the U.S. had dropped two atomic bombs on Japan during World War II, we were taught that this horrific act was justified because it led to the surrender of Japan and an eventual end to the war. The U.S. had been the only power to possess nuclear weapons until the Soviets developed the technology. The two countries became enemies in a new kind of battle called the Cold War. Both countries were strengthening their arsenals and could annihilate one another. Our disaster drills at school were practiced, not only to prepare for bad weather, but also for a possible attack from Soviet missiles. The drills would have us scrunching down underneath our desks with a book over our heads. During the Cuban Missile Crisis, I remember being quite scared and wondering what the world was coming to. President Kennedy had given a speech to the public in 1962 describing pictures of Soviet Missiles in Cuba that were pointed at the U.S. I thought we were going to be in a nuclear war with the Soviets, and the school's disaster drills were obviously not going to save us! I remember going to bed one night in the middle of this crisis and wondering if I would be alive the following morning. Luckily, Cuba agreed to dismantle these missiles and a major conflict was averted. Life was back to normal in Western Springs!

Fortunately, another facet of the Cold War was evolving between these two mega-powers: space travel. The Space Race officially began in 1957 when the USSR placed the first satellite, Sputnik, in space. The Soviets continued to be winning this race for several years. They sent the first man into space on April 12, 1961 to fully orbit the earth. Twenty-three days later Alan Shepard, a U.S. astronaut, accomplished only a sub-orbital mission. After almost a year after Shepard's mission, John Glenn successfully completed a full orbit for the U.S. At school, we were so thrilled to be witnessing these events, and we knew that our country would eventually surpass the Soviets.

In the classrooms, we would often watch these missions on a TV that was wheeled into the room, or sometimes we would just listen to the events through the intercom system. We were just happy to have our regular routine of bookwork be interrupted with such exciting news! It seemed like we were catching up to the Soviets' superiority. President Kennedy gave the famous "Man on the Moon" speech on May 5, 1961 which announced our goal of placing a man on the moon by the end of the decade. This plan had seemed like such a futuristic notion, but now this impossible dream was going to happen in my lifetime. The lunar missions were being planned and a tremendous amount of money was allocated for these endeavors. Most importantly an exciting new era had begun between two major superpowers who were fighting for superiority without using traditional, destructive methods. It certainly was a hopeful time!

Chapter 9

High School Begins

In September of 1963, my high school experience began at South Campus of Lyons Township High School, or LT, and I was full of anticipation. LT was one of the largest high schools in the state with an enrollment of five-thousand students. I wanted to get involved in new activities and meet more friends at this impressive setting. First thing on my agenda was to try out for the freshmen cheerleading squad. The high school cheers were a different style than the ones from junior high, and I did not master this "fine art" as well as many of the other girls in the competition. There were more than two-hundred girls at tryouts, and I did not even make the first cut. What a disappointment! Now it would be harder to be popular and well-liked in high school!

Then I tried to get involved with some clubs, but I found most of them rather boring except one called GAA, Girls Athletic Association. This organization provided girls with intramural types of activities such as volleyball, gymnastics, basketball, and modern dance to name a few. It wasn't anywhere near as "cool" as being a cheerleader, but it gave me a way to expel some of my pent-up energy. This outlet was desperately needed after sitting in uncomfortable desks all day. (There were dress codes in public high schools in those days, and girls were not allowed to wear slacks. So, we usually wore sweaters with skirts. Either we had bare legs and socks, which were not so cool, or we wore stockings with a girdle or garter belt. Those undergarments were really uncomfortable for our rear ends that were planted on hard school desk chairs!) There were no competitive sports for girls then. We could only choose from cheerleading, pom-pons, and GAA for a form of physical activity. Pom-pons were not open to freshman girls, so GAA was the only option. It definitely wasn't very "hip" but it was the only game in town and was better than nothing at all.

I thought I was going to make a lot of new friends from the other feeder schools, but I found that process slow indeed. In fact, I actually became closer to an old friend from my junior high instead. This girl's name was Carolyn. I don't remember how we had become so close that year, but we began talking on the phone every night. We discussed all the important issues, which usually involved what cute boys we had encountered that day.

High school dances were another thing to look forward to, or so I thought! The first big dance of the school year was the Homecoming Dance. A boy named Jerry (this name should have been red-flagged for future reference) asked me to go to the big event with him and I immediately gave my consent. I felt that since he was the first one to ask me, it was the right thing to do. (I had probably read too many teenage romance novels.) Jerry was a couple of inches shorter than me, and even worse, he was skinnier too. I bought a dress and had shoes dyed to match, which were the MOST UNCOMFORTABLE SHOES EVER! His dad drove us to the decorated gym where we would be lost in a sea of mostly upper classmen. We attempted to dance a few slow dances and walked around the circumference of the gym trying to find other couples as uncomfortable as we were. Finally, the night was over, and Jerry's dad pulled up his big sedan to take us home. Thank goodness it was over. I no longer liked my rule of saying "yes" to the first boy who asked me out. I'm sure Jerry didn't have such a great time either. I decided to figure out a nice way of getting myself out of questionable situations, but I really didn't know how to come up with excuses without hurting someone's feelings. However, I knew that I did need to work on some sort of strategy!

Close to Valentine's Day, there was a girl-ask-boy dance every year called The King of Hearts Dance. Carolyn and I decided to take the plunge and muster the courage to ask dates to the dance. I asked Bob and she asked Steve. We were so excited during our nightly phone conversations in anticipation of the big event. This dance had to be different than Homecoming since **we** asked the boys that **we** had crushes on. And Carolyn and I had each other to talk to if things became awkward. Well that dance wasn't any better than my former experience. In fact, it was probably worse. The boys probably would have preferred watching a chess game on TV than being at this dance with us! After that awkward evening, I continually felt uncomfortable when Bob and I would cross paths with one another. And it seemed like it happened all the time, even when our high school days were long over. Isn't it odd that such insecurities during adolescence can continue to haunt us? Even at my twenty-five year reunion from high school, I still felt awkward around him. Maybe we should have acknowledged the situation right away, laughed about it, and moved on. Another lesson to be learned: our expectations are usually greater than the reality. Freshman year was really just an extension of junior high, only on a larger scale with more opportunities for me to mess up. My first year in high school was definitely not what I had imagined. The dances were pretty disastrous and being one student in a huge class was certainly a big adjustment. It was a transitional year that taught me to have a little more patience with life and not to expect so much from others.

XXXXXXXXXXXXXXXXXXXXXXXXXXXXXXXXXXXX

There are a few events that happen during one's lifetime that will never be forgotten. November 22, 1963 was one of those days. While eating one of my favorite cafeteria lunches, the eight cent meal of mashed potatoes and gravy, I heard someone at my table say that she had heard a rumor that President Kennedy had been shot. The girl sitting across the table from me laughed and clapped her hands thinking that it was probably a joke. The Chicago suburbs were considered a Republican stronghold and the Democratic President was not a popular person around the neighborhood, except with Catholics. They were delighted to have the first person in the Catholic faith to become president. However, no matter what your political persuasion, no one wanted the President of the United States to be harmed! I had thought that such types of violence occurred only in unstable countries; not here in America! There was no official announcement for us students at school, which I think, in retrospect, was a huge mistake. We had the right to know about something so horrific, but in those days anyone under the age of twenty-one had few rights. One of my friends proceeded to ask one of the teachers supervising the lunchroom if the rumor was true. He simply nodded his head solemnly in response. I didn't find out more details until later when I returned home from school.

President John F. Kennedy, or JFK, and our First Lady, Jackie, were riding in a convertible during a parade in Dallas, Texas. A gunman fired some shots from a building along the route and hit President Kennedy. The media rapidly speculated about whether he was truly dead or not. Later the official word was given that President Kennedy died from an assassin's bullet. During that week, all three major television stations, ABC, CBS, and NBC, covered nothing but that tragic situation and the funeral of our thirty-fifth President. Vice-President Lyndon Johnson was immediately sworn into office: our country had a new leader.

It was a very somber time and in order to escape some of the constantly depressing coverage on television, Dad decided it was time to look at our home movies. He had an eight millimeter film camera, without sound, and he had filmed our vacations, birthdays, holidays and special events. Our normal routine was to watch each movie reel right after it was developed, and then each film would be stowed away in a drawer and pretty much be forgotten about. There were no movies on video or digital recordings to watch: we only had a black-and-white television with a handful of stations that could be tuned in with an antenna. So we made the best of a bad situation and reminisced about the good times we had had as a family by watching these old films. Later in the 90s, I had the old movies transferred onto VCR tapes so we could use the technology of the time to look back at our earlier lives. I gave my brother and sister each a copy of the tape for posterity's sake.

Looking back at my freshman year, I realize that 1963 was a pivotal year in America, when we learned that we were not isolated from violence. Our leaders were extremely vulnerable and there were more killings of influential, powerful people yet to come in the decade. The 50s had seemed to me like such an innocent time period; but now, as I was growing up, I was becoming more aware of the "real" world with complex issues and problems. Not only was I becoming less naïve about the world around me, but so was the nation as a whole.

Chapter 10

And the Beat Goes On

(Sung by Sonny and Cher in the 60s)

The British Invasion had begun! Rock-and-roll bands from England were providing the popular music for teenagers. Some of my favorites were The Kinks, The Rolling Stones, The Zombies, and the best of all was the Beatles. This type of music had a whole new sound and we could not get enough of it! We wanted our music to be new and different, and it certainly was! *I Want to Hold your Hand* and *I Saw Her Standing There* were a couple of the Beatles' first hits. We would play the hot songs of the day at one another's homes, at slumber parties, and at The Corral, a place where LT students could hang out on weekend evenings. We had small transistor radios and would listen to Chicago AM radio stations: WLS, WIND, or WCFL. If a slow ballad would come on when I was alone in my bedroom, I would pretend I was dancing with a cute boy like the kids did on the TV show, American Bandstand. It was fun to have a little fantasy and wind down from school before getting to my homework which I usually begun right after dinner.

When summer finally arrived, I hung out at the local swimming pool in Western Springs. I became good friends with a really nice girl, Lois. She was the epitome of what it meant to be "cute" in the 60s. She was about 5 foot 2 inches tall, had long blond hair, and a nice figure. The boys always noticed Lois, even though she never seemed to think she was anything special. She was always laughing about something, especially her comments about her older brother, who was a bit different. Maybe we had those "big brother" annoyances in common, but I think we mostly both just respected each other a lot and enjoyed each other's company. Since Carolyn was not a member of the same swimming pool, she and I were beginning to drift apart that summer. I was just learning the fact that changing friends was a normal progression in life: people come in and out of your life when situations change.

Once sophomore year began, Lois and I agreed to share a locker together. Each of us at LT was provided with a locker, but we decided the coolest location would become our shared hangout. We picked the locker that was nearest the gym and boys' locker rooms: that way we had a better chance of seeing the jocks who were going to practices right after school. It's sad to admit, but my friends and I were totally boy-crazy. It was also fun to decorate the inside of our locker door with pictures of our favorite rock stars: especially John, Paul, George, and Ringo. Every girl had her favorite Beatle and mine was Paul: he stole most teenage girl's hearts back in the sixties.

During sophomore year, some of our friends were turning sixteen: the magic number to which everyone looked forward. A driver's license was the coolest thing that anyone would acquire in high school. It meant total independence; as long as your parents allowed you to use their car! You could always tell when someone had just obtained his/her driver's license because that person would be constantly jingling and holding the keys up like they were a trophy. And the best news about our ability to drive ourselves around the area was that you could now go to a school dance without having a parent take you back and forth.

Lois was starting to date a guy named Dick, who was one of the lucky ones to have an early birthday. I met a boy named Laird who I thought was a pretty smart guy, and he was one of Dick's friends as well. Laird was in the advanced classes at school, and I admired his intelligence. I respected his opinions on some of the hot topics of the day, especially politics. Before Laird and I began dating, he had dated a girl, Jaki, who lived in my neighborhood. She had gone to the Catholic grade school, so we never went to the same elementary school together and did not know one another very well. One day as I was walking home from high school, I saw Jaki just ahead of me, so I caught up with her to ask her about what she thought about Laird. She said he was a nice guy, but she was no longer interested in him. Little did I know at that time that Jaki was about to become my next best friend and that Laird, initially, would be our common link.

Now in October of '64, my immediate concern was getting ready to go the Homecoming Dance with Laird, who had just asked me to go with him: I had to get a new dress. I was also excited that Dick was able to drive our little group to the dance. We had a great time and went to Johnnie's Pizza after the dance. It was located in LaGrange Park and had the best thin crust pizza around the area. Our group was sitting around the table looking at the pizzas we had just ordered, one of which had small meatballs on top. We girls were all decked out in our fancy dresses, trying to look sophisticated, when Lois proceeded to pick up a slice of a meatball pizza. And then one of the meatballs dropped down the front of her dress. We could not stop laughing! She must have been a little embarrassed but it was so very funny. So much for being polished and refined! Now school dances were really becoming a fun time! I was part of a nice group of friends and we enjoyed each other's company. And having a member in our group with a driver's license was so totally cool. Dick later had a party at his house, and his parents actually left the home to us for a couple of hours! I was certainly surprised that his parents were so trusting! We played romantic music, like Chances Are by Johnnie Mathis, and slow danced by rocking back and forth in each other's arms to the dreamy music.

Then a few weeks after Homecoming, Dick's father, who was only forty years old, died very suddenly from a heart attack. We were all shocked that one of our friends had lost a parent. Dick must have felt totally abandoned and seemed to have difficulty dealing with his despondent mother. Shortly thereafter, he would become very possessive of Lois and wanted to spend all of his time with her. She had a hard time saying no to him since she knew what a difficult time this period was in his life. He did not want her to spend much time with us girls and used the excuse that she would be so much safer with him. It seemed that he was insecure about her possibly meeting another guy that was more popular than he was, and that he could lose her. He continued this controlling behavior all through high school and even into college. They would eventually get married while attending University of Illinois. But a possessive relationship usually doesn't work out, and theirs was no exception. They divorced one another after a few years. Lois and I had remained friends in high school, but we were not very close any more. I resented Dick's neediness and Lois' inability to be independent. As sophomore year continued, I became better friends with Jaki, and she had a whole group of new acquaintances to add to the mix. And so, the beat goes on!

Laird and I continued to date throughout sophomore year. However, I was not very assertive in our relationship. He was not the type of guy to call on the phone very often:

he thought it was a waste of time. He also did not give me much notice about going to some of the dances during the school year. This behavior was particularly rude since I had to figure out whether I needed to buy a new dress for each occasion. Mom was pretty good about the last-minute shopping and didn't complain, probably because she was happy that I was enjoying my social life. Laird was starting a pattern of taking me for granted and I should have had the guts to stand up to him. Jaki would encourage me to refuse one of these last-minute invitations from him, but I wanted to be part of the social scene, and so I would cave in and accompany him to the event. Even though I would scramble to get my act together, I usually had a nice time. Later that summer, Laird would go away to camp and the time apart was just what I needed to set my priorities. At the end of the summer we broke up, but we managed to remain friends throughout the rest of high school. The only down side to the new direction in my life was that Lois and I would not have as much time together. There was no more double dating, and I missed our close friendship.

Sophomore year was definitely my favorite year in high school. My group of friends was expanding and I really enjoyed all the social events. I started to become a better student academically too; my grades were improving and my teachers seemed to like me a lot. I guess I felt like I was fitting in. And I was learning another one of life's lessons: that things that are important to us just take time, so have a little patience!

Chapter 11

Getting Down to Business

Lyons Township was divided into two separate campuses that were about a mile apart from one another. The more recently built South Campus, for freshmen and sophomores, was located near our subdivision so I could easily walk to and from school everyday. However, the campus that was dear to our hearts was the beautiful North Campus where juniors and seniors were educated. It had all the charms of an older building. This reddish-brown brick building was so picturesque with the old clock tower surrounded by mature trees which were especially colorful in the fall. The football field, across the street, hosted many decades of battles with other teams from the suburban conference. Unfortunately, years later, that beautiful football field would be demolished and replaced with more classrooms, and the new field would be built back at the South Campus. Some of the tradition and charm would never be the same.

Homecoming week was a particularly eventful time. Each school club as well as each class had a float to build for the parade. It was the one of the few times that we were allowed to be unaccounted for on a school evening. Usually, we were to be at home on these school nights unless a student had a part-time job. I was not expected to work after school: luckily, my parents thought my studies were time consuming enough for me. So for spending money, my parents continued to give me a small allowance of $2.00 a week, but I did supplement my limited income with babysitting jobs in the neighborhood.

I turned sixteen years old at the end of sophomore year, but did not pass my driver's test until the beginning of my junior year. After a second try, I was given the coveted award: my driver's license. Now I was one of those girls who could jingle my keys everywhere I went to prove how mature I was. My parents were pretty liberal about letting me use one of the cars. I have to give Dad a lot of the credit in making me feel so confident about my driving skills. He had taken me to a cemetery to practice my turns, parking and so forth. He even fell asleep next to me when I was driving to the South Side of Chicago on the Stevenson Expressway even though I was driving only with a permit. He was a good driver, so I think he thought I would be one too. However, I was never allowed to take the car to school for daytime classes, nor did I expect to do so. Now Jaki and I would have to take the bus to North Campus. We were at the "cool" campus but it was over a mile away from our houses. I learned how long and boring riding a school bus could be: it was only a smidgen better than walking.

Once most of my friends and I had received our driver's licenses, we became instantly "too cool" to simply hang out at the teen-center, the Corral. So we would often "cruise" Macs (McDonald's) and Tops (Big Boy Hamburger Restaurant) on Friday nights attempting to meet other teenagers and determine if any parties were going on in the area. Usually, none were to be found, so we would continue "cruising" LaGrange with the radio blaring singing along to our favorite hits. It was especially fun when Sara would drive since she had a big station wagon that could hold quite a crew of us. Besides Jaki and me, our group had now widened to include Sara, Judy, Pam, Mary, and Nancy. We spent many hours looking for fun and excitement, but actually found our own good times together within the confines of the vehicle.

During junior year, I became a lot more serious about my academics and I was proud of my grades: mostly A's and B's. My favorite subjects were German and Chemistry because I respected the way both teachers organized their classrooms. Mr. Hoch, my excitable German teacher, gave me a lot of attention, which I thoroughly enjoyed. He made a rather mundane subject an interesting experience, and because of him, I would join the rather nerdy German Club. My old-fashioned chemistry teacher, Mr. Craven, had extremely strict standards in his science room. He demanded that his assignments be done every night. If homework was forgotten, a student would be humiliated in a sarcastic, but humorous way. That student would be told to get out a piece of paper and to copy this dictation, " Dear Mommy, I did not do my chemistry homework last night. Please sign this note and return it to school." It was so totally cool when the big jocks had to put their cocky heads down and follow Mr. Craven's instructions. Everyone would be snickering around the room. So I made sure that I always did my homework particularly in that class since I did not want any negative attention. Most of these "cool" guys eventually started to appreciate Mr. Craven's wit and sarcasm, and his classroom would become one of the favorite spots to hang out before school. He made a challenging subject seem comprehensible if you followed his example and worked hard. It was one of the few subjects in which I received straight A's, and he gave me the confidence to pursue a major in science when I went to college.

Another popular high school activity in which girls could belong was being a member of the Pom-pon squad. LT had only one squad, a varsity squad, and only two girls made this prestigious group during my sophomore year and I was not one of them. It was at this time that my focus had changed from wanting to be a high school cheerleader to becoming a pom-pon girl. This activity involved incorporating dance steps along with the movement of colorful pom-pons to band music. The kick line was always a crowd pleaser too, when the audience would quite often stand and cheer. So, I had hoped to make the squad my junior year, but again, no such luck. My only consolation was that I was one of only ten junior girls that had made the final cuts. At least I knew that I was close to making the squad, so I did not stop trying. At the end of junior year, tryouts for the following year's squad would be held. I copied the tryout music on a reel-to-reel tape machine so that I could practice the dance steps over and over again. I was determined to make this squad my senior year. And, my persistence paid off! I was one of ten senior girls who made this elite group. I was thrilled. Although, it was a shame there were not more enjoyable activities for girls in 1966. There were approximately five hundred girls in my senior class and only a handful of us was able to take part in popular activities. Thank goodness, Title IX came along in the 70s and created new opportunities in academics and athletics for girls and young women!

Chapter 12

A Few Detours

During the summer between junior and senior year, I decided that it would be fun to find an out-of-state summer job. I applied to work at different camps and vacation hotels all over the Midwest. I landed a job in beautiful Lake Geneva as a waitress and cabin cleaner. The pay was miniscule but the opportunity to live and work away from home was invaluable. There were about thirty teenage girls who lived in an old dorm with a house mother and father to watch over us. There were also about eighteen boys that lived right next to us in the boys' dorm. Even though we had curfews to observe, we felt so independent to be living away from home for the summer. The girls' lounge was located in the back room in the dorm, and we listened to records and smoked cigarettes. Our favorite music that summer was the Mamas and Papas album, *California Dreaming*. We played the songs over and over again, singing along with all the words while puffing away on Kool, Tarryton, or Marlboro cigarettes.

While I was away, Mom would send me some nice long letters about what was happening at home. I now cherish those letters since they reflected some of Mom's thoughts and ideas at the time. If I hadn't gone away to camp that summer, I would never have had those special mementos. And my sister, Cheryl, who was just seven years old at that time, would send little notes or even a drawing to me as well. Being in Lake Geneva for the summer was an escape from the normal suburban lifestyle. Unlike my friends back home who were complaining that they were bored with nothing to do, I was having all sorts of new experiences. (They probably needed to get a job!) But, even though I didn't make very much money at camp, I felt privileged to have this experience.

Dad worked at Bell and Howell Co., a large firm that manufactured movie projectors, cameras, and ditto machines. Even though Dad was one of the men that lived the farthest from the plant, he was one of the first to arrive at work every weekday morning. And, he was also one of the last workers to leave for home as well. He enjoyed commuting to work on the newly constructed toll ways. The construction of interstate highway system began in the late 1950's due to the Cold War. These highways were built to become a means of efficiently moving military equipment. But the unintended result of these roadways was that Americans could now commute father distances to and from work as well as the ability to travel all over the country more easily. When Dad had landed the job at Bell and Howell a couple of years earlier, we did not have to relocate and move to a new home, as he was willing to drive the 45 minutes each way to and from work.

The first few years that Dad was employed with this company, he was thrilled doing the work that his job required. His title was Director of Manufacturing, an upper management position. However, a couple of years later a new boss arrived on the scene and Dad was becoming concerned about the security of his job. This man was very impressed with the younger, college graduates that were starting new careers with the company. Gradually, Dad was beginning to lose his confidence in his ability to fulfill his work obligations, and this insecurity lead Dad to become depressed. Mom was very supportive of her husband and always had the attitude that everything would turn out for the best. Dad began to seek professional help from both a psychiatrist and our minister. He tried some medications, mostly tranquilizers, but these drugs seemed to just make him tired and did not lift his spirits. To make matters worse, Grandma was now living with us so Mom and Dad did not have much privacy. Mom began working part time at the church so she could get out of the house for a couple of hours a day. Dad would often come home from work, go directly to his bedroom, and just sit and stare into space. The whole family tried to be positive and encouraging, but he was clinically depressed, and he was going to need more help than just our good intentions.

In the beginning of my senior year, Dad was admitted to Lutheran General Hospital by his psychiatrist for depression. But the stress of being in the hospital made Dad very nervous. He did not want anyone at work to know that he was being hospitalized for a mental illness. So he never filed the bills for his hospital stay with his insurance company and instead paid these bills out of his personal account. In the 1960s, there was a lack of understanding from the general public about clinical depression. The ward that Dad was assigned had people with severe mental illness and he felt very uncomfortable there. He was depressed but not psychotic! Needless to say, this experience only made his anguish worsen. He was released from the hospital after a few days and was told if he were to return to a hospital setting he would need electric shock treatments. That extreme measure seemed like it was the only option left. I think Dad had made up his mind that he was not returning to a place with a bunch of crazy lunatics and ineffective treatment options.

My coping mechanism for dealing with the somber tone around the house was to stay as busy as possible at school and with my social life. I continued working hard on my classwork and was very surprised when I was elected to

National Honor Society during my senior year. I think I had a couple of teachers who were really instrumental in sponsoring me to become a member of this prestigious group, since there were many kids much smarter than I that did not get elected to NHS. But I was a hard worker and eventually graduated in the top 16 % of my class.

I loved being on the pom-pon squad that year and especially, wearing my uniform to school on most Fridays! We performed for all the home football and basketball games, the Homecoming Parade, and the State Street parade in downtown Chicago. After that activity was over, I enjoyed being involved in a production called the Corral Show. I was part of a chorus line that had an equal number of guys and girls dancing together. We were the eighteen-ninety bathing beauties; that's the only time I have ever been a bathing beauty! It was fun teaching the guys how to do simple dance steps and eventually performing in front of the student body, parents, and friends. To end my senior year, there was prom, held in the ballroom of the Sherman House, one of Chicago's impressive downtown hotels. After sewing my own dress, I went to the dance with a very nice, platonic friend named Bob. The following day we headed over to the sand dunes on Lake Michigan which was just under two hours away. And of course, I thought I was going to get a golden tan in a single day: **not** with my light, freckly skin! I did manage to turn a pretty bright shade of red for graduation which was held a couple of days later.

I had applied to two colleges and was accepted at both. Initially, I planned on going to University of Iowa to enroll in the Pharmacy Department, but later decided that the in-state tuition at University of Illinois would be a better choice. The least I could do for my family was to try to ease as much of the financial strain as possible. Both

Mom and Dad were one hundred percent behind me in my decision to advance my education. They would have been very disappointed if Dad's illness kept me from entering college. During my senior year, I also began working a part-time job as a cashier at Walgreen's Drug Store earning $1.50 per hour. I decided to continue working there during the summer and saved as much money as I possible could. It wasn't as much fun as the previous summer at Lake Geneva, but being financially responsible made me feel like I was contributing to my future.

Chapter 13

A Rough Start

Mom helped me prepare for my journey to the big campus in Champaign, Illinois. Dad did not feel up to traveling with us. We packed up the car with many of my belongings, and I headed to college to become a coed living in a dorm on campus. One of Dad's biggest regrets was that he never finished his mechanical engineering degree. He had taken night classes while working full time and eventually received approximately two years of college credit. I was amazed at how fast he could read the material in an engineering book. However, he felt he wasn't fully educated since he did not have much background in the liberal arts. There were times that I wished he would have quit his stressful job and gone back to college to earn that degree. Such an idea would have been highly unusual during that time period: a person over the age of forty did not go back to college.

Even though I was worried about Dad, I was so excited to live on campus. I had quite a few other friends that were going to U of I, but I didn't have any idea who my roommate would be. Fortunately, I was assigned to a small dorm room in Illinois Street Residence Hall and met the person that would share my dorm room: Joanne from a Catholic Chicago high school. She was a petite Italian girl and was one of the sweetest persons I have ever met. Another acquaintance from high school, Linda, was assigned a room just two floors below us. The three of us would become the closest of friends during our freshmen year. I was very concerned about how well I would do academically at the big university. Luckily, Lyons Township High School did a great job preparing me for the challenge of college-level classes.

Joanne, Linda, and I would meet at the adjacent cafeteria to our dorm in the evenings to engage in some silly behavior and tolerate the "fine" cuisines prepared by people in white coats. We also ventured out to a couple of freshmen mixers to try to meet other coeds, but decided these planned events were pretty much a waste of time. Once freshmen orientation week was over, we became busy with our studies and serious socializing remained a weekend activity. Being freshmen girls in 1967, we had curfew restrictions. At midnight the main entrances were locked, and a girl could be in quite a bit of trouble if she tried to enter the building "after hours." One evening, Linda did not make curfew, so she called to us from the courtyard below. Our window was wide open since it was still warm in Champaign and we could easily hear her high-pitched voice pleading for help. We decided that Linda could sleep on one of the couches in the unlocked lounge on the first floor if she was given a pillow. She could then wait until morning to enter the dorm and not face any consequences for being late. We threw a bed pillow out our eighth floor window. What a loud thud it made on impact! Linda jumped backwards and screamed. Joanne and I were in hysterical fits of laughter! We might as well have opened one of the exits in the basement and set off the alarm, all of which would have been far less noticeable. So after the pillow episode, we decided that the next time one of us was late, opening the exit door was definitely a better plan as long as we ran immediately back to our dorm rooms. Lucky for us, our sneaky little trio never did get caught being tardy. We thought we were so very clever! Such silly types of behavior were common occurrences for us. My introduction to campus life began with many light-hearted experiences: however, for me, the situation was about to change.

One evening in late September, a counselor from the dorm's front office brought me downstairs to a conference room. She told me that there was someone from home waiting to see me. I knew that this was not how we typically received a visitor from home. I had a queasy feeling in my stomach thinking that something was seriously wrong. I tried to console myself that maybe something must have happened to Grandma. She was elderly and had already had two heart attacks, so for those few minutes, I was bracing myself for some bad news about her. Upon opening the conference room door, I saw a man whom I recognized immediately as Mr. Ramcke, very good friend of my parents from church. Now I was praying that the news was not about Dad; it had to be about Grandma! I sat down next to Mr. Ramcke, and I heard the words that I dreaded, that Dad had passed away earlier that day. No one had to tell me what had happened: I knew Dad had taken his own life. Mr. Ramcke had used some lame excuse that he was in the Champaign area on business. But I suspected that he had made a special trip to give me the news in person and help me return home safely. He would wait for me to pack a suitcase and I'd be on my way back to Western Springs.

That drive home seemed like the longest three hours of my life. I just sat in the back seat and wiped the tears away that were falling down my cheek. Dad had mentioned earlier that he had felt that he would be better off dead than alive. All of us, except Cheryl who was too young to understand, had tried to convince him that his self-worth should not defined by his ability to earn a paycheck. But not being able to support his family was unthinkable to him and any type of welfare or public assistance was too degrading to accept. He had also focused on the possibility of losing his home which he thought would be totally devastating. Even though he had been suffering from a depression, he still retained all of his fiscal intelligence. He knew if he died that the loan on the house would be paid off due to mortgage insurance, his life insurance policies would pay Mom a lump sum, and social security payments would help her with incidental bills. Since he was so tormented by his own pain, he could not imagine the loneliness and empty void that Mom, Cheryl, Vernon and I would experience due to his final decision to take his own life. People considering suicide can not fathom the hurt and emptiness loved ones will have to endure from such a decision. It is said to be a selfish way of dying, but when someone is so despondent, that person cannot reason beyond his or her own issues. Loved ones of suicide victims always regret that they could have done or said something to save that person's life. I thought maybe I could have said something to help him conquer his feelings of inadequacy. It took me years to accept the fact that all of us did the best we could to help Dad, and we were not able to save him from the many pressures that had accumulated throughout his life and pushed him over the edge.

Little did I know when I began my college career, that my academics would not be my biggest issue I would face. It certainly turned out to be a bittersweet time in my life.

Chapter 14

Too Much for Grandma

After a week of being away from college, I returned to my classes a bit stunned. A loss of a loved one takes months to fully understand, which is nature's way of helping us cope with the tremendous stress on the body. My immediate concern was to make up the schoolwork that I had missed. It was difficult for me to tell each instructor that my father had passed away. But I needed to communicate to them that I planned on doing whatever was needed to complete my work during my absence. Some of my classes were so large that there was actually no need to share my personal information with the head professor, since he or she did not know who I was anyway. I talked to each instructor or teaching assistant that would be assigning me my final grade. Missing a week of school was a big deal since there was a lot of work given out each day in my classes.

Now there was no reason for mom to still care for Grandma, so she went to live with her last living child, Uncle Elmer, in Milwaukee. After a month or two, he and his wife, Marge, realized that they were overwhelmed trying to care for Grandma in their home and found a nursing home for her. In the 1960s, there was a negative stigma placed on people who sent their relatives to any facility that cared for the elderly. Some ugly things were said by Grandma's nieces about Elmer's decision to "send Grandma away for their convenience." However, Grandma's health had begun a downhill slide: she was losing her will to live. I'm sure this new living arrangement was the right place at that time in Grandma's life.

Reaching old age can certainly be a difficult task, since one may experience so many hardships over a long life. Grandma lived a tough life beginning with immigrating to a new country as a young girl. I have no knowledge of her early developmental years in Germany, but it must have been difficult to leave one's friends and many family members to travel across the Atlantic Ocean to an unfamiliar land. Most of the immigrations in the late 1800's were for economic or religious reasons, and I suspect that hers was the latter. Even though her hope was to live a better life in America, she certainly experienced tremendous obstacles in her pursuit of happiness. Losing two school-age children so prematurely, witnessing the suicide of her husband in her own home, and then being present when her youngest son at the age of forty-seven committed suicide would certainly turn even the most positive person into a bitter one. German women have been known to be strong-willed, but everyone has his or her breaking point. At one time I resented my grandmother for being so self-centered and controlling, but now I only feel compassion for a woman trying to do the best she could. She certainly had many faults but she tried to focus on the good qualities in her life such as her talents of cooking, baking, cleaning, and crocheting. A year after Dad's death, Grandma's heart finally gave out, both literally and figuratively. She was laid to rest next to her husband in Evergreen Park Cemetery back in her long-time home in Illinois.

Chapter 15

Back to Normal?

Returning to the routine of college was the best medicine for my mental health. After seeing what Dad went through during the end of his chosen vocation, I was more determined than ever to find a career that would be as far away as possible from the business world's pressures. It made sense to me to pursue my degree in Secondary Education of Biological Sciences. If I had inherited any of Dad's genes that affected my emotional well-being, then a career in a recession-proof field that would also provide me with tenure seemed like a good fit. So working hard on my studies gave me purpose as well as an escape from the grieving process.

My social circle was certainly broadening, but Joanne and Linda were still my closest friends. I did not feel comfortable sharing Dad's choice in the way he ended his life with many acquaintances, only with my closest friends did I share those details. If I needed to I comment that he had passed away, I would continue discussing my concerns for Mom and my eight-year old sister, Cheryl. By my changing the subject ever so slightly, I helped to steer people's curiosity over the details of Dad's death in another direction. And I wasn't stretching the truth: I was truly deeply concerned over Mom's and Cheryl's mental anguish.

College weekends were full of social events, which I enjoyed, but with some guilt over the worry concerning the situation at home. The local college bars would serve beer to us coeds, even though we were not yet the legal drinking age of twenty-one. The older college guys liked to flirt with us innocent freshmen girls, and we enjoyed the attention in return. But every few weeks, I would return home to spend some quiet time with Mom and Cheryl. During the first year after Dad's death, Mom was pretty despondent. Cheryl would now sleep in the other twin bed in Mom's bedroom at night, which I think gave both of them comfort. Later, Cheryl told me that she does not remember much of her third-grade year when she was absent from almost one-third of the school term. Quite often, Cheryl would complain about a stomachache, and Mom would then keep her home. I'm sure that Cheryl did have a nervous stomach in the morning after hearing Mom cry so much at night.

Raising Cheryl was now Mom's priority, which was a good mental place for Mom to be giving herself time to heal from such a horrible ending to her marriage. It took her a couple of years, understandably so, for her to feel positive about life again. Mom had "bought into" the suburban lifestyle of being a typical contented housewife of the 50s and 60s. She enjoyed her role as wife and mother; she was not terribly interested in pursuing a career. As a result, she did not have much of a back-up plan when life turned on her so cruelly. So for the next couple of years, her role was to be exclusively Cheryl's mom, which was probably the best scenario for both of them.

Dad's suicide left me feeling very empty, hurt, and sad. Even though I knew this desperate act was not anyone's fault except Dad's, there was always a nagging feeling of regret thinking "if only" I could have said something that would have changed his unbalanced way of thinking. Mom must have reflected on a lot of "what ifs" too, since she was the closest person in Dad's life. But she had felt firsthand how difficult it was to reason with an extremely depressed person. She could not have tried harder to be more supportive or helpful during Dad's illness. We were all doing the best that we knew how; it just wasn't enough to shake Dad of his demons.

By the end of my first semester at U of I, I met a junior named Jerry. I was certainly not the most emotionally stable person after Dad's death, so I was looking for a boyfriend to ease some of my loneliness. Our first "date" was really quite a disaster. I had actually been on a date with another guy at the local college bar, Kams, that evening, but my eyes had been flirting with a guy who was pouring beers to customers socializing in the basement of this establishment. When my date left to use the restroom, Jerry and I began a quick conversation and had agreed to meet at midnight to go to another party. So I accompanied Jerry to an overly-crowded gathering that was held in an apartment somewhere off campus. Since every room in this small place was jammed with people, there were plenty of conversations to be had throughout the whole apartment. I had been talking to some guy whom I barely knew in one of the back rooms when I realized that my "date" had left me there in disgust. I guess Jerry was mad because I wasn't spending all my time talking to him. So I was left in quite a predicament since I had no means of getting back to campus. Eventually, when the party ended, I talked this same guy into giving me a ride back to my dorm. Still another complication of being a freshman was that I couldn't enter through the front entrance until several hours later. So I waited around until the doors opened for normal morning operations. I was so tired when I finally arrived in my dorm room that I slept most of that Saturday. But I had left my hat in Jerry's car, which I wanted to reclaim. I called his fraternity house and talked to him the next day to ask if I could to pick up my lost item and apologize for being so rude by ignoring him at the party. Instead of my seeing a red flag concerning **his** irresponsible behavior, I was accepting the blame for the unpleasant situation!

Our first "date" had turned out to be a pretty good indicator of how the relationship would later develop. Since I was emotionally the needy one and wanted to avoid confrontations, I usually took responsibility for most problems that arose in the relationship and was the first to apologize. I wanted a strong male in my life so I continued to date Jerry exclusively. I was not yet strong enough to set proper boundaries and to be my own advocate; my emotional baggage was too great for me to see that I could be happy alone and without a boyfriend. So I continued being in a relationship that lacked the nurturing I was really seeking.

xxxxxxxxxxxxxxxxxxxxxxxxxxxxxxxxxxx

The week before second semester was about to begin, the sororities traditionally host a series of parties in each house to recruit girls to become members. Over a period of several days, each girl would eventually list the top three sororities that she would consider pledging. My first choice was Phi Mu and I was absolutely thrilled when I was extended an invitation to become a member of that house. The Phi Mu house was a beautiful structure and had a good location on campus. But more importantly, I thought the mood of the girls in the sorority was very upbeat, and they seemed to be genuinely nice, interesting young women. At first, Mom was a little apprehensive about my joining a sorority, thinking it would be a snobby organization of spoiled college students. But she changed her mind when she had visited campus for a U of I mother's weekend and really liked the respect the sorority girls were showing for one another as well as for their moms. A sorority house was certainly a more comfortable lifestyle than the impersonal dorm: the food and study areas were so much more adequate. And it seemed like being a member of Phi Mu would certainly help my self-esteem issues. The only concern that I had was the segregation of race and religion that was apparent throughout the Greek system of fraternities and sororities. Certain houses were labeled as either Gentile, Jewish, Black, or White. At least Phi Mu seemed fairly progressive for that time period with a mix of Jews and Gentiles. So I thought that Phi Mu would be a good fit for me, and I was so glad that they thought I would be an asset as a member of the sorority house as well!

As important as it was for me to be accepted into a sorority, the "real" world was engulfed in many serious issues of which I was becoming more aware. Even though there were many causes that seemed unjust in 1968, the United States' involvement in the Vietnam War and the lack of equal rights for women and minorities were the ones getting most of the attention on college campuses. Protests and sit-ins were common scenes when I would be walking to my classes in various buildings on campus. I was a little too naïve at the time to become involved with any of the protests, but I was beginning to learn more and more about these political and social issues. And a rather major incident occurred late that spring semester: Martin Luther King, Jr. was assassinated in Memphis on April 4, 1968. Dr. King was the leader for civil rights and advocated nonviolent means, such as protests or sit-ins, to spread the word of the discontent over unfair treatment of minorities. Especially in some areas of the South, Negros were discriminated against by not having choices in pursuing education, jobs, housing, and the right to vote in public elections. So when Dr. King was killed just outside a motel that he and other civil rights workers had been staying, the word spread like wildfire. Unrest erupted throughout the nation, and rioting and looting were predominant scenes on the television news coverage. The inner cities were affected the most with the destruction of businesses that were mostly in poor areas. Being a student still living in the dorm, we were not saturated with much news since there were few televisions to watch on campus. But we were totally aware of the violence throughout the nation from other media outlets such as radio and newspapers. Even though I did not witness the destruction first hand, I knew that the mood in the country was becoming more and more violent.

Chapter 16

Continuing Education

Over the summer of 1968, I was fortunate to land a good-paying job with International Harvester Company so I could save as much money as possible for college. Mom paid my tuition, room and board, but I had to pay for almost everything else. Clothes, shoes, phone, and travel expenses were all my responsibility. I was grateful for Mom's generosity in paying my main college expenses since I noticed that many of my friends had to work part-time jobs while going to college to ease the burden of costs to their families.

Before I left school for summer vacation, I knew that my roommate in the sorority house next fall would be Bonnie, a rather conservative, attractive, quiet girl from Mundelein. We decided to meet over the summer to do some shopping at a brand new indoor mall, Randhurst. The location was approximately halfway between our homes, and I thought it was a pretty cool, new trend of having all the stores under one roof. Little did I know then, that I would spend a lot of time shopping in this mall later in my life, since I would live just a few minutes away. And that ultimately I would witness the eventual destruction of this old, outdated structure in my lifetime. For now, Bonnie and I enjoyed our day together and we picked out some cute matching bedspreads for our shared room in the sorority house.

I was so looking forward to going back to school and not having to explain to Mom where I was going all the time. Once you feel the independence of making your own decisions, it's hard to live under someone else's roof. So Mom and I had a few misunderstandings that summer; she was probably just as glad to see me go back to college as much as I was to leave.

Another political event happened that summer that continued to prove the volatility throughout the nation. On June 5, 1968, Bobby Kennedy, the brother of the former president John Kennedy, was assassinated while campaigning for the Democratic nomination for President of the United States. He had just finished a speaking engagement in a California hotel and announced that his next stop would be Chicago. When he was leaving the reception room in that hotel, he was gunned down by Sirhan-Sirhan, a deranged man affiliated with a rather radical political group. It seemed like this violent act was another setback for the Civil Rights Movement. Bobby Kennedy had been a huge supporter of equal rights for minorities, especially for the Negroes. His death had many people who were looking for change in America very distraught. At one time the proper term for African Americans was "Negro" instead of "colored", but now a new label was emerging to properly identify this minority: Black would become the proper term be used in this country to identify this race for the next twenty years. And much later, another politically correct term for Blacks would be added: African American.

Before his death, Bobby Kennedy's popularity had been climbing in the polls, and he probably would have been the nominee for the upcoming Presidential election. Now it appeared that Hubert Humphrey was leading candidate for the Democratic platform. As many as ten thousand demonstrators were heading to Chicago to protest the Vietnam War and the leaders of this movement planned on getting some television coverage to boost the awareness of the anti-war sentiment. As my summer was winding down, the Democratic Convention was about to be held at the Amphitheatre located near downtown Chicago from August 26 – 29. Mayor J. Daly was very angry over the fact that the protestors picked **his** city to use as a platform for protests and possible unrest. So he requested twenty-three thousand police and National Guardsmen to keep the "Hippies" and other protestors far away from the convention activities. The news media were covering the stories occurring outside the parameters of the convention where protesters were having ugly and violent confrontations with police, all of which were being documented on television news broadcasts. The disgust with the Vietnam War was now given more credibility due to all the media coverage. It would be a long time before either political party would venture back to Chicago for a convention after airing around the world the chaos and turmoil that occurred that August.

When I returned to campus a few weeks later, there was an even more serious tone about politics than seen just a few months earlier. Some of my sorority sisters were involved with the upcoming Presidential campaign, and there were always interesting discussions around the dinner table. Even though I wasn't yet old enough to vote, I was finding the amount of energy given to political causes an interesting phenomenon. There was a lot of passion surrounding so many issues in 1968, and I knew that I had a lot to yet learn about them. But the one that was beginning to interest me most was that of women's rights. However, with a new year of school beginning, I was back in my own little world focusing on continuing my studies at the University of Illinois.

Quite a few Phi Mus, including Bonnie, were biology majors like me. Since the course load was fairly rigorous, all the bio majors had each other for support to navigate our way through understanding the content. Most of us were quite concerned about passing a prerequisite class, Physics. With so much the time spent in my lab, quiz section, and lecture classes, I felt I was pushing myself to the maximum to earn decent grades. However, another opportunity presented itself to me that I couldn't resist. Tryouts were being held for a brand new pom-pon squad that would perform at football and basketball games. One of the girls that engineered the whole idea of starting a new squad at U of I was a former high-school classmate of mine. We had both been members of the high-school squad together. The tryout routine was choreographed with many of the same steps that I had learned in high school, so I definitely had an advantage over many other girls. And after a series of tryouts, I soon learned that I was selected as a member of the newly formed squad, The Illinettes. This new status gave me a great boost to my delicate ego and made me feel that I was belonging to a rather elite group on campus.

Jerry and I were still dating seriously, even though it was a relationship full of drama. Most of the turmoil came when he felt that he was being ignored or that I was paying too much attention to someone else. My grades were important to me, so I spent a lot of time studying, and being on the pom-pon squad was a major time commitment as well. The older girls in the sorority also wanted us pledges to attend parties with different fraternities. So there certainly was a lot of pressure on me for my precious time. If Jerry sensed that I did not put him first, he usually became quite aloof and would begin to withdraw. I hated conflict and I would usually apologize so the relationship would stay in tact.

As second semester rolled around it was the beginning of 1969 and there seemed to be a change in priorities for young people throughout the nation. The "sorority" scene was becoming less important to me as well as it was to many of the older girls in the house. They were moving out to apartments and living more of a "hippie" type of lifestyle. The whole look for young women was changing to a more free style of having long straight hair, no bras, and loose, casual clothing. The protests on campus over the Vietnam War were heating up quite a bit and were hard to ignore. I was often surprised by how many of the boys on campus were not very concerned over their grades. If a guy flunked out of college, he would lose his student deferment and would be drafted into the army within a very short time. Some young men were burning their draft cards in protest of the war and there were others that were even moving to Canada to avoid being forced into combat. Even though the voting age in 1969 was twenty-one years old, an eighteen year old was old enough to lose his life in a war that many believed to be unjust. Our parent's generation could not understand all the unrest. World War II had been a popular cause, and many from that generation were disgusted by the young people who protested our government. Women were not part of the draft: only eighteen-year-old males had to register and could be told to report to duty if their precinct needed more men to serve in the military. It now occurred to me that important issues were now much bigger than my own limited environment.

Right after Easter break, I was starting to feel more independent and was having second thoughts about continuing such a serious relationship with Jerry. But we were still seeing one another when in late April my menstrual period was over a week late and I wasn't feeling very well either. I went to the college clinic and the doctor told me that I would need to wait a couple of weeks to have a pregnancy test. In those days, there were no early pregnancy tests available to a woman. Abortion was not yet legalized so I felt I had two choices if I were indeed pregnant: to get married or have the baby as an unwed mother. My girlfriend, Linda, had just had a baby out-of-wedlock and she decided to raise her baby boy by herself. I thought she was very brave to handle such a tough situation, and since her parents were very supportive, she had chosen not to give up her baby for adoption, as many young women would have done in those days. But Jerry and I decided to get married the next week before any medical tests could be performed to confirm a pregnancy. We felt that we did not want people to think that we "had" to get married, so we eloped on May 2, 1969 and got married in Urbana's City Hall.

I did not feel that I could initially share my predicament with Mom, but I eventually told her that we had eloped. I did not share any information regarding a possible pregnancy. I'm sure Mom suspected something was wrong, and I knew I had hurt her by not including her in such a major decision with my life. But there was also a possibility that I was not pregnant, or maybe I would have a miscarriage in the first couple of months of this pregnancy. So why should I have to admit that I had made a huge mistake? I was trying to deal with the hand that I had been dealt, and I thought, at the time, that if Jerry and I both tried very hard, we could make a marriage work. Since my parents always had respect for one another in their marriage, I thought it would work for me too. It seemed like the right solution to an immediate problem. When spring semester was over, Mom gave us a party during summer to celebrate our marriage. I think she felt like she needed to do something. Plus, since she had given many nice wedding gifts to other friends and relatives, she felt that I also deserved some nice things from her friends. I was certainly uncomfortable with my whole situation, but I was trying to make the best of it for everyone, and most importantly for a possible new baby.

Jerry and I were now a married couple going to summer school in Champaign. He needed to take three more classes to get his degree, and I wanted to accumulate as many hours as possible. So I enrolled in two difficult classes: genetics and field botany. Since I did turn out to be pregnant, I was pretty tired and drained but was trying to complete all my class work in the summer heat of central Illinois. We lived on the second floor of an old house with no air-conditioning. One of the highlights that summer was when my professor brought to class nine puppies that were absolutely adorable. It was pretty easy to talk Jerry into adding another member to our family, so we adopted a light tan mutt and called her Poochie Dog. She turned out to be a medium-sized, short-haired dog with a sweet temperament, and a great companion for me.

Another major event happened that summer, which fulfilled the promise that John F. Kennedy had made nine years earlier. July 20, 1969 was a monumental moment in America's space program. Apollo 11 was to land on the moon and the first steps could be witnessed by everyone who owned a television. Since we did not have such a luxury item, we joined a group of other students and enjoyed watching the surreal experience in a friend's fraternity's living room. We cheered when the fuzzy black and white picture of Neil Armstrong stepped down from the ladder and placed the first foot step on the moon's surface. As he was planting his foot on the surface of the moon, he said something, but the reception was not very clear. Later, I learned he had said, "One small step for man, one giant leap for mankind." Watching that snowy picture on the television was a moment in time that I will never forget. The modern age was here at last!

Chapter 17

A New View

When we finished the summer school term in 1969, Jerry was now a college graduate and could begin earning a living. We moved to Des Plaines and he began to look for work. However, he had also lost his college deferment and would be reclassified as 1A, which meant that he could be drafted into the army. To avoid that possibility, he considered enlisting into the Navy's program for aspiring pilots. He took some aptitude and medical tests, and the latter test informed us that he had some early signs of diabetes. He would not qualify for the Navy's program, but he could still be inducted into the army. During this time, however, President Nixon changed the entire system that determined who would and would not be drafted in the military. A lottery was going to be held based on possible inductees' birthdays to determine who would be drafted. If a guy lucked out with his birthday falling on a high number in the lottery, the odds of his getting drafted were very slim. Jerry was blessed with the luck of the Irish in the lottery, and he received a high draft number. He did not need to entertain any more ideas about enlisting in the Armed Services and could concentrate his efforts on looking for a decent job in the Chicago area.

I had enjoyed college life immensely, but now I needed to transition to becoming a responsible adult. The baby was due in the beginning of January, so I didn't have much of a choice but to wait around the house while Jerry worked. I took an adult-education class in knitting. Since this new skill was all I had to occupy my time, I became a knitting maniac. That Christmas I made four sweaters, a cape, and several scarves, mittens, and booties. I was looking forward to having the baby, being less dependent and working part time or going back to school. My life was now so totally different than just a few months before.

On an extremely cold day in early January 1970, I gave birth to a baby boy, Jerome Thomas III, or JT. The big event happened on Jerry's dad's birthday, so he was given a special birthday gift of being a first-time grandfather. Having a baby changes your whole life. Not only did I need to worry about myself and my husband, but I had another helpless human being to keep happy and healthy. Luckily, JT was a very good baby so I felt very thankful. He was not cranky and as a newborn slept quite a bit. But I was getting bored and after a few months, I would look for a part-time job to help supplement our income.

We rented an apartment in Wheeling and our rent was $170 a month, which Mom thought was a lot of money to waste on rent. She had mentioned that she would help us with a down payment if we decided to look for a home to buy in the future. But for now, I landed a waitress job just a few miles away from our apartment and that income gave us a little extra spending money. Jerry found a job that required him to travel quite a bit, which probably helped us stay together and avoid conflict. Our communicative skills were pretty lacking and I was not a very happy person. My waitress job helped me meet some people my own age in this new environment. Life was better now that I was busy as I liked getting away from the isolation in the apartment, especially since a newborn baby does not provide one with much stimulating conversation. I felt the important responsibility of being a mother, but I truly missed the good times of being a regular student on a big college campus with an important goal of getting a college degree.

I was determined that my goal was merely being put on the back burner and eventually I would obtain my college degree!

Chapter 18

Spring 1970

Protests against the Vietnam War were constantly aired throughout the news media. Even though I was not part of the college scene, I was aware that the unrest all over the country had elevated substantially since I had left college. Occasionally, the National Guard needed to be called to assist the police in areas that were on the verge of violence. There was a strong underground movement developing, especially on college campuses, which had the potential to be quite dangerous. One group, called The Weathermen, was responsible for bombing one of the buildings at the University of Wisconsin, but luckily, no one had been injured from the blast. However, on May 4, 1970, a student protest at Kent State University in Ohio over The Vietnam War was getting very nasty with hateful comments being exchanged back and forth between students and police. The Guardsmen were brought to campus to try and settle things down. Instead of a calming effect, however, tempers flared and gun shots were fired. It was reported that sixty-seven rounds were fired in a thirteen-second time period killing four students and injuring nine, one of which suffered permanent paralysis. It appeared that the violence of the Vietnam War was now felt firsthand on ordinary college campuses.

This tragic event sparked horrendous revolts all over college campuses nationwide due to the tremendous disgust over the "establishment" controlling young people's lives. There was such chaos that most schools chose to shut down operations several weeks early rather than chance such an event occurring on their own campus. Students were told to go home and grades would be determined based on the work that previously had been done that spring semester. Ironically, the aim of these protests was to promote peace, but it led to a situation of twenty year olds killing other twenty year olds in our own backyard instead of Southeast Asia.

Even though I was concerned over the horrific event that happened to the Kent State students, I had already made plans to go out a couple of days later to celebrate the coming of my twenty-first birthday. Jerry's mom was willing to babysit and we went out with a small group of friends headed for an evening of bar hopping. I would turn the legal age exactly at the stroke of midnight, and I was ready to receive my free drink from each establishment. It was a celebration of adulthood for me: I was now old enough to legally drink alcohol and vote in national elections. Although with every birthday that I celebrated thereafter, I would sadly remember the Kent State students, many of whom were my same age that had died so tragically in 1970.

My life, however, was going to take a positive turn. Mom, who had been working only temporary jobs, had offered to stay home and babysit JT for the summer if I wanted to enroll in a summer school program. Cheryl was too young for Mom to leave her alone all summer so Mom decided not to take on any employment that summer and would watch my six-month-old baby while I attended classes. Returning to a college atmosphere was right up my alley! University of Illinois had a "sister" school that was located near downtown Chicago. It was called Chicago Circle. It was such a relief to know that my son was in good hands with Mom, and I could continue working on my goal of receiving my bachelor's degree. This university was composed of mostly concrete buildings and sidewalks. It had a much colder atmosphere than the beautiful campus in Champaign which had unique buildings of different architectural styles along the shaded quad in the center of campus. Students at U of I Circle were all commuters and would leave campus as soon as classes for the day ended; therefore, seeing a protest was a rarity. There were very few parties, no sororities, no college bars, no Big Ten games – just classrooms, study areas, and cafeterias. However, I also did not have the time for many frivolous indulgences. Commuting, working part time, motherhood, and studying filled my days that summer. So this school suited my basic need of earning my teaching degree. The final process would take a little bit longer than I had previously planned, but I felt my life was back on track. There was a dim light at the end of a long tunnel!

Chapter 19

Mission Accomplished

After finishing my summer school experience at U of I Chicago Circle, I realized that the majority of the workload towards receiving my degree was finished and I did not want to stop the momentum of accumulating college credits at this time. By carefully planning my class schedule, I could attend classes three or four days a week which cut down on my time commuting. The money I earned as a waitress would cover the expenses of tuition and babysitting. So I decided to enroll as a full-time student during the fall of 1970 and found a young mother to babysit JT while I attended school. Trying to be a good mother to a very active toddler, working part time as a waitress, and squeezing in enough time for my class work were all distinctive challenges. But this hectic routine seemed more rewarding as I felt so much more productive with my life than the year prior. The next spring semester was a continuation of the same routine of studies, work, and motherhood.

In addition to balancing school and motherhood, Jerry and I now became homeowners. Mom had thought that renting an apartment was a waste of money, and she supported us in our decision to purchase a home. With her generous loan of $11,000 for a down payment, we bought a three-bedroom split level in Mount Prospect. We paid $33,000 for a fourteen-year-old home in a neighborhood full of families with young kids. Our monthly payments were approximately $250 including taxes! Mom was right: it was a very good investment! Housing prices rose quickly for the next few years, so we were very happy with our decision to become homeowners.

The following fall semester, I began my student teaching at nearby Arlington High School. Instead of spending at least an hour and a half commuting to and from the city, I now could drop JT off at the babysitter's house and be at school in twenty minutes. What a relief! I taught freshmen biology and worked with great teachers in the high school's science department. I felt that this career choice was the right one for me, and I hoped to acquire my own teaching position in a few years when JT was of school-age himself.

Jerry's job entailed quite a bit of traveling, so we were together primarily on weekends quite often working on projects around the house. Since I was still waitressing, we were not spending a lot of time together on those weekends. However, we managed to conceive another child that winter, just as my student teaching semester had ended. Two children was my idea of a perfect family, and my kids would be less than three years apart in age. I was hoping to have a daughter since I was already experiencing raising a son and did not expect to have any more children down the horizon. Of course, my main concern was to have another healthy child, whether it be a boy or a girl. After a couple of months into my pregnancy, I decided to quit my waitress job and concentrate primarily on finishing my college work. I now only had one semester left to complete all my requirements. In June of 1972, I received my degree in Biology Education. What a relief! I was rather proud of the fact that I was only one year behind the more customary schedule of completing a college degree within four years.

Labor Day in 1972 was a very special day for me. The holiday lived up to its name: I started having labor contractions that morning. The pains were becoming closer and closer together so Jerry drove me to Lutheran General Hospital in Park Ridge that afternoon. That evening I gave birth to a beautiful, eight-pound baby girl, Jennifer Joy. What a relief: to have another healthy child! It was customary in those days for women to be detained in the hospital for three days, which for me was entirely too much time. I felt great and wanted to get home to my normal life. After plenty of rest, Jenny and I were released from the hospital, and JT was finally able to meet his new little sister. JT had always found babies to be quite fascinating subjects, and his little sister was no different. He did not harbor any jealousy and seemed to enjoy sharing the limelight around the house with his little sis. I felt very thankful to be blessed with having two healthy children.

Even though I had encountered quite a detour to my original plan when I started college in 1967, I was proud of myself that one of my most important goals of receiving my college degree was fulfilled. I never wanted to be totally dependent on anyone again for my emotional or financial wellbeing.

Chapter 20

A Change in Direction

After almost a decade of news coverage concerning the Vietnam War, President Nixon announced to the nation that our military would end offensive operations against North Vietnam. I was shocked that this frustrating, long-lasting war was suddenly over! Our country had been involved in this conflict throughout all my teenage years with no clear end in sight. Years earlier, President Johnson and his advisors had known that this war could not be won. But he did not want to have a lost war on his record. Instead of dealing with this unpleasant situation, he decided not to run for another Presidential term and acknowledge the change in the nation's sentiment over the conflict in Southeast Asia. As a result, the war continued for several more years until the Nixon administration, wanting to stay in power, realized that a change in our military strategy needed to occur.

Sadly, over 58,000 United States' soldiers died over the course of this war and many, many more Vietnamese had been killed. It was a major relief to me that this horrific war was over and the voices of so many young people had finally been heard by our rigid government. However, many civilian demonstrators had focused a lot of pent-up anger at the soldiers, who had been engaged in fighting in this unpopular war, instead of towards the policy-making government officials. These soldiers should never have been blamed for carrying out their military orders. When these men returned after serving in the war, they were ignored instead of honored for their service. There were no parades for them as there had been when World War II had ended. Many Vietnam Vets had a very difficult time adjusting to life back in America where the tone in the country was now one of mistrust in our government.

The rest of the 1970s was not a time for much national pride. President Nixon resigned from office in disgrace after being involved in a major cover-up of illegal practices regarding his upcoming campaign. This incident was known as The Watergate Scandal, which seemed to confirm the suspicion of unethical behavior concerning our governmental officials. Time was needed for the nation to heal from so much discontent and to move in another direction. For the most part, student activism would become a relic from the 60s and early 70s. The voting age would change to eighteen years old for national elections and military service would become one made up exclusively of volunteers: the draft would not be reinstated. The atmosphere on college campuses would become far less politically charged and much more complacent. Protests, sit-ins, and lively debates would rarely occur around the country after the mid-70s. With the controversy ending in Southeast Asia and more personal freedoms given to young Americans, the atmosphere throughout the rest of the country seemed to quiet down as well.

Chapter 21

Life Goes On?

After delivering Jen into the world in 1972, I realized how beautiful the month of September could be! I had always associated this time of year with spending so much time indoors instead of being able to enjoy one of the best months of the year. Most September days in the Chicago area are of moderate temperatures with little humidity, and my garden would reap the benefits by overflowing with luscious vegetables such as tomatoes, green beans, zucchini, and cucumbers. Gardening was an activity that I really enjoyed especially since I continued to have a lot of time to myself: Jerry's job still entailed a lot of travel. We were not an emotionally close couple since we were just busy with raising children, working around the house, and making ends meet. Our social life was primarily one of separation. He would often go out to bars and I would like to hang out with neighbors or a girlfriend. I also began waitressing parttime again which helped me feel connected to other people my own age.

Even though my marriage was not a very satisfying one, I remained busy with the normal routine of life. In 1973, there was quite a January thaw when the temperatures in the area reached the 60s. It was a nice break from the cold winter days that we had been experiencing. The morning of January 25th, I had begun my usual routine of making a pot of coffee, giving JT a bowl of cereal, and strapping Jen into a high chair where she could place one or two Cheerios into her mouth. (Of course, our dog Poochie was eager and willing to clean the floor from the falling little O's underneath the high chair and loved to slurp any milk that remained in JT's cereal bowl.) Both kids needed a mid-morning nap, so after putting them down to bed I began my work around the house. Jerry was out of town for the week and I only had my two kids and myself to worry about.

Later that morning the phone rang. I was surprised to hear my brother's voice on the other end of the line. He and his wife, Pam, had temporarily moved in with Mom so they could reduce their expenses and return to college. Mom was usually the one to call me, not Vernon, and she would have been at work at College of Dupage at that time in the morning. In the first few seconds of our phone call, I was trying to imagine what my bother needed to talk to me about. I would find out soon enough. He didn't beat around the bush; he immediately blurted out that the Mom had been in a car accident on her way to work that morning. Unfortunately, while making a left-hand turn, Mom hit a patch of black ice and lost control of her car. She slid across the center medium and into oncoming traffic. She had always worn her seat belt, but the '67 Mustang did not have a shoulder restraint: it only had a lap belt which did not protect her. Her car was hit a couple of times before it came to a stop. Mom was in bad shape and died in the emergency room at a nearby hospital. Hearing all this horrible news was totally shocking and unbelievable! Mom had finally started to get her happy personality back and was enjoying her life of working and taking care of Cheryl. After hanging up the phone with my brother, I immediately thought of my sister, Cheryl, who was only in eighth-grade: she was now an orphan. At least I was an adult who should be able to take care of myself, but what was going to happen to Cheryl?

Before driving over to Western Springs, I called my best friend Jaki, who told me not to attempt to go anywhere in such a frame of mind. She would come out, pick me up and then bring me to Mom's house where all the relatives had been gathering. Mom's brothers must have done most of the organizing for Mom's wake and funeral; I don't remember very much since I'm sure I was in a state of shock. But I do remember feeling that life seemed very unfair to me at this time. How could God have taken her away from us? Mom was just starting to turn her life around and she needed to be there for my sister! I learned quickly that there are no guarantees in life. Mom had always said that the good die young, and I never thought that those words would apply to her.

Even though Mom's will and testament listed her older brother, Jim, as guardian for Cheryl, we all agreed that it would be better for Vern and Pam to take over the responsibility of raising my sister. They were all living in Mom's house and Cheryl could stay in the school and neighborhood that felt most familiar to her. The next few years would be hard on all of them, but most difficult for my sister. The best that I could do for her was to be a good listener with her frustrations of dealing with such sadness and loneliness. In hindsight, counseling would have probably been a good idea for all of us but most importantly for my thirteen-year-old sister. On the surface, she seemed to be adapting fairly well by confiding in her best friend and her mother when things got difficult for her.

We were all doing the best we could to get through a tremendously stressful time in our lives. I felt some consolation knowing that Mom had had the opportunity to experience being a grandmother to both of my children. Even though I was technically a grown-up at the age of twenty-three, I resented the fact that my adult relationship with my mother, that had recently just begun, was now over. She was only fifty-two years old and was taken from us way too soon. Her home had always been the main family hub for holidays and celebrations, but it would no longer be a place of family gatherings. Vern and Pam were putting in their time to raise Cheryl until she would graduate from high school. The house in Western Springs did not feel like a home any more without Mom's presence. Once Cheryl graduated from high school, the house was sold and everyone went separate directions. Vern and Pam moved to New Jersey and Cheryl found an apartment in a suburb nearby to the only home that she had ever known. Life was not what I had imagined it to be like just a decade earlier, but I had to learn to deal with feelings of emptiness and provide a loving home for my own children. As the old saying indicates: "Life must go on."

Chapter 22

Restless

Even though my life had been radically changed around by my mother's death, I noticed that being around JT and Jenny could not keep me in total sadness for long. They were both very happy, content children and their giggles and smiles lifted my spirits. I did some soul searching and was beginning to realize that I was living in an empty, unhappy marriage and felt that there should be more fulfillment in a relationship. I was not thrilled of becoming identified with the stigma of being a "divorcee." However, with Mom gone, I now had no one else to disappoint if a change in my life was needed. I wasn't making any decision immediately, but was beginning to consider that divorce might be a possibility in the future.

Jerry was ready for a change in his career. He had yearned to be his own boss so he dabbled in some side jobs in the hydraulics' industry. During this process, he stumbled upon a small plastic-injection molding business that was for sale. We scraped together enough money for him to take over this small business, and he quit his secure sales job that had quite a few nice benefits with it. This career change meant no steady paychecks, no health insurance, no company car and no plan on how to pay the bills. I decided to increase my hours as a waitress and to update my resume and look for a teaching position.

When I began my college experience in 1967, teaching jobs were widely available. However, now in 1974, many baby boomers had been graduating in mass numbers with teaching certificates and most of the teaching jobs were drying up. These positions were now difficult to find, but luckily, I was a science major, and there were still some opportunities available in that field of study. I interviewed for a freshmen biology job at Arlington High School, but that position was only for a one-year leave of absence, and it would have required an additional time commitment of coaching as well. I decided that a junior high program might be a better choice for me since the pressure to coach would not be as strong. My valuable time at any school could only be used for my classroom teaching and not for extra-curricular activities. I knew if only I could find a teaching job, I could pay most of the household bills and have health insurance for the whole family. It was time for me to roll up my sleeves a little sooner than I had previously expected and find a full-time job to support the family.

Chapter 23

Sandburg

It was the middle of August in 1974 when I entered Palatine School District 15's personnel office. After a brief meeting with Paul Young, Director of Personnel, I agreed to continue interviewing for a science position while traveling in his car. Paul wanted me to meet a certain principal at one of the schools before he left for the day. Paul had already received my records and recommendations that I had previously dropped off at the office. I was surprised by this method of interviewing, but classes would be starting in a couple of weeks and the last few positions needed to be filled quickly, so I was agreeable to this unusual request. As we pulled in the driveway of Carl Sandburg Junior High, I remember thinking, "How great would this place be? It's the closest school in the district to my house and would only be a short daily commute for me!"

We entered the building together and I met Dan Vucovich, a nice-looking man in his mid-thirties. We discussed a few educational issues concerning methods of teaching and discipline techniques. But my having two small children at home could be considered by many potential bosses as a liability for becoming a good employee. In 1974, many women with children stayed home until her youngest child went to school full time. Another challenge to working outside the home was good childcare was not easy to find, but first I needed to worry about landing a job. Financially, I did not have the option of staying home any longer and was eager to begin my career. Dan questioned my work ethic by pronouncing, "You can't call in sick just because you cannot find a babysitter." And I responded, "During my student teaching semester, I had not missed a single day even though my son was only a one-year- old at the time." Then I proceeded to listen to Dan expound upon his philosophy of education for about fifteen minutes. Luckily, I didn't have to say very much and just needed to nod my head in agreement now and then. Next, Dan suggested that we look at the science classroom, which was quite a large room with three rows of old black lab tables and a demonstration area towards the front. Then after walking back to his office, he suggested that I discuss the job position with my husband and to let Dan know my decision tomorrow. I was shocked: he just offered me a teaching job! Was that all there was to the interviewing process? Whew! I wanted to tell him right there that I would take the position, but I managed to stay composed and shook his hand before leaving his office.

The next day could not come soon enough when I could seal the deal: I would be a full time teacher in a nice neighborhood near my house. My starting salary was $9,000 a year which included health insurance for me. For an additional fee, I could cover the whole family in the district's health insurance plan. What a huge relief!

Next on the agenda was for me to find a dependable babysitter. My neighbor, Rosie, told me that her sister-in-law, Mrs. Scaletta, might be interested in babysitting, and she lived only a couple of miles away. Her youngest child was just entering kindergarten and she was interested in earning some extra cash by working at home. I offered her $50 a week, which was a generous sum to watch two children, and she accepted the weekly salary. It was such a relief for me to know that my kids had such a responsible caregiver in a loving atmosphere while I was away at work.

JT and Jenny also had the opportunity to experience what life in a big family was like since the Scaletta family, with five kids, totally absorbed my kids into the fold. My guilt of having to leave my young children while I went to work was significantly reduced by knowing they were in such a nice environment. I knew that I was very fortunate to have found this wonderful home for them in which to feel welcome.

My rookie year of teaching was a difficult one indeed. I had no concerns over the science curriculum, but issues of discipline were definitely my problem. I needed to learn how to deal with the junior high mentality; this process took me quite a while to figure out. Luckily, I got rehired for a second year and my confidence in classroom management was continuing to improve. I definitely was getting a handle on the tricky business of disciplining this age group. My principal wanted the classrooms in his building to have few behavioral problems from the students and even fewer complaints from the parents. My goal was to concentrate on improving my ability to manage the classroom effectively, so I would receive tenure the following year.

The staff at Carl Sandburg was mostly made up of young teachers and there were numerous opportunities for social events throughout the school year. Even though there were days that some of the teachers would go out for a drink together after school, I usually needed to get right home after school to pick up Jen and JT from the babysitter's house. They needed to get home as soon as possible to their own environment with their neighborhood friends. However, to feel that I was contributing to the overall atmosphere in the school, I would volunteer to help with every evening dance or other school events. I also enjoyed meeting the group of volunteers for a cocktail or two somewhere nearby when our chaperoning services were over. It was important for the staff to be able to vent frustrations to one another over the pressures of the job since no one else really wanted to hear the issues of dealing with junior high students! And as teachers we were so isolated from other adults during the teaching day that contact with one another was very important for good morale.

With two years of teaching completed, I received the coveted level of tenure in my teaching career. Achieving that signification boosted my self-confidence. During my teaching day, I was feeling more and more fulfilled, but I began to dread my weekends at home with my aloof husband. We didn't have huge fights or arguments, but instead we would go for long periods of time without talking to one another. At first the lack of communication would bother me, but I eventually became accustomed to this kind of neglect. Jerry would often go out to a bar in the evening and I was just as happy to be left alone. It was just a matter of time before I faced the real truth that the marriage was disintegrating.

Sandburg became my second home and gave me a feeling of having an extended family. Many ups and downs in my personal life happened during my thirty-two years of teaching at Carl Sandburg, and due to the close camaraderie of the teaching staff I felt empowered to weather many storms. My closest friendships were developed in those smelly halls and cramped, smoke-filled lounges. In retrospect, I feel I lucked out with the best possible profession and school for me to develop the self-confidence and emotional wellbeing that I gained as I matured into true adulthood.

Chapter 24

Single

After almost two years of on and off periods of separation in our marriage, our divorce was granted on February 23, 1978. One of the main concerns had been over child custody arrangements, but we finally agreed upon joint custody of our children. Even though this type of legal agreement was quite unusual in the late 70's, the Cook County judge who was presiding over our case agreed reluctantly to grant this new type of arrangement of sharing the time equally between both parents. At the end of the proceeding, she admonished us against returning to court for every disruption and disagreement that may occur in the future. Normally, the custody of the children would be awarded to the mother, and the father would have visitation rights only on weekends. Since Jerry had been extremely persistent on pursuing this new, more equal arrangement, I was willing to give it a try. However, I insisted that we needed to live within the boundaries of the same school district, so that JT and Jenny could have access to both homes whenever necessary. We set up a schedule of the kids staying at one home for an entire week, and on Sunday evening, they would relocate to the other parent's home. We also agreed to sell our marital home, split the equity, and find new places to live in the Mt. Prospect area.

I knew that on a teacher's salary, I needed to find the most reasonable place that I could find. So, once a good offer came through for the sale of our marital home, I placed a bid on a small ranch house that was only three blocks away from our old neighborhood the kids loved so much. I was very happy with this basic three-bedroom brick home, even though it only had one bathroom and no basement. It was the right location for the kids and me. However, obtaining a mortgage would prove to be another ordeal. Even though I had had a stable job for over four years and had come up with a down payment of more than fifty percent of the home's value, the loan officer at the local bank was not confident that my mortgage would be approved. His concern of my credit-worthiness was over the fact that I was a woman! Single women were considered to be a risk factor for procuring a mortgage in the 70s, and even a married woman's income would often not be considered when a married couple was trying to purchase a home. The banking industry felt a woman might become pregnant which could result in the loss of her job. Quite often, an employer would fire a woman if the knowledge of her pregnancy was known. But luckily, my application for a $30,000 mortgage was approved, probably because I had such a healthy down payment. Thank goodness the local bank was willing to take a risk on me. Now I was eager to begin heading in a new direction.

Jerry found a split-level home about a mile away from my little ranch. The kids felt relieved that they were able to have both parents active in their lives, even though we lived in a community where being a child of a divorced parent could attach somewhat of a stigma to it. But this arrangement was the best possible one for us: it certainly was not ideal, but it was manageable. We continued to adhere to the conditions of joint custody in the divorce agreement for the next few years, which luckily kept communications between Jerry and me to a minimum. Finally, the tension that I had felt for so many years was now lessened and a more "normal" routine was about to begin.

Since I now had more free time than before my divorce, I needed to expand my interests and also seek out new friends who were in similar situations. While attending a social group for young single parents, I met a nice woman named Debbie, who was also a recently divorced mom. We became good friends for the next several years and were able to understand each other's frustrations over dealing with issues concerning our ex-husbands and raising kids. When the spring arrived, we decided to take golf lessons together as well as plan a couple of weekend excursions at nearby locations.

One Friday evening in late September of 1982, I was enjoying an evening of playing poker with some friends at Debbie's apartment. JT and Jenny were staying at their dad's house, so I wasn't worried about my being out a little late. It was probably just after midnight when I arrived back home and shortly thereafter went to bed. JT had told me earlier that evening that some of the local kids from the Catholic school had been doing pranks around the neighborhood. I wasn't too concerned since the pranks were basically silly things like ringing someone's doorbell and running away. I liked having a little fresh air in the house and had a couple of windows cracked open very slightly.

Even though I had just fallen asleep, I thought I heard an unfamiliar noise coming out of JT's bedroom. So I arose and walked towards the source of the noise: it was one of the windows that I had left cracked open. Thinking that the neighborhood kids were now doing a little caper at my house, I walked right up the pane of glass to tell them to get off my property. However, instead of seeing some young teenagers running around my yard, I saw the face on an unfamiliar, white male looking right at me as he was cutting through the window screen in my son's bedroom. I yelled at him to leave me alone as I pounded my fist on the window. The glass broke and cut the inside of my wrist. Immediately, I ran to the phone and dialed "O" for the operator. There was no "911" service available in our area at the time. Before I could hear a voice on the other end, the intruder managed to run around to the front of my house, break the small pane of glass in the door, drop his arm through this opening and unlock the doorknob. I couldn't believe how fast everything had happened! He was now coming towards me in my own home: how violated and frightened I felt! I dropped the phone and struggled with him for a couple of minutes. He must have seen the phone dangling by its cord, so he went over to it and hung it up. Now I thought that I was doomed since my connection to the outside world was disconnected. I decided to make a run for the front door. He grabbed me before I could get outside and threw me down to the floor. Miraculously, the phone rang! He looked at me, realized that someone knew that something was wrong, and immediately ran out of the house. I quickly answered the phone and heard a voice identifying himself as a policeman who was inquiring if everything was all right. I blurted out that I had just been raped and to please come over as soon as possible. Technically, I had not been raped since no penetration had occurred, but I knew that I had been assaulted in my own home and understood exactly what the perpetrator's intentions were. Within a few minutes of receiving that welcomed phone call, the police were at my front door. They searched the area and listened to my account of what had just happened. I was taken to the emergency room at our local hospital, was given a complete physical, and received some stitches on my right wrist. That scar has never left me, and has been a constant reminder that as a woman, I need to be so very careful about my safety.

I wondered what had alerted the police to call my home in the middle of the night that evening. I had assumed that a neighbor had heard my screams, but that was not the case. Months later, I learned that my original call to the operator eventually did get answered after I had dropped the phone. The operator had heard much of the struggle that was going on between the perpetrator and me before he had hung up the phone. She summoned her supervisor, was able to determine my address, and contacted the Mt. Prospect Police. One year later, I had the opportunity to meet this person, who had used such good judgment, at an award celebration being held in her honor. Due to her quick thinking during my attempt to reach help, she had qualified to receive the life-saving award the phone company annually awarded to employees that had fit the criteria for intervening to save someone's life. I was so thrilled to have the opportunity to meet this person who had been so perceptive when receiving my call and did not dismiss the sounds that she had heard on the phone as something unimportant. When I actually had the pleasure of meeting her, I was surprised at how similar we were to one another. She was my same age, had been divorced earlier in her life, and also understood how careful women needed to be.

The Mt. Prospect Police were very helpful in trying to solve my case. They asked me to look through many mug shots of criminals that had recently been in the area, but no one looked familiar to me. I had no idea who this person could be, but wondered what I might have done to provoke such an attack. I pondered whether the type of clothing that I had recently worn or if places I had been could have called some unintended attention to me. But deep down in my gut, I knew that this guy had the problem, not me. His plan that evening was to rape me, which I knew without a doubt because he had indicated his intentions with some very colorful language. Fortunately, no sexual violation had time to occur. I never felt very comfortable in that house again; I always had apprehensions over his possible return.

However, after I had a little time to think things over, I decided that I would not let some maniac determine the direction of my life. I decided to make modifications to my home so it would be a more secure place to live. After all, it seemed like a very safe neighborhood with very little crime around this area of suburbia. I replaced my front door with a new steel structure, had floodlights installed on each corner of the house, and placed wooden bars in each window. Unfortunately, JT and Jenny were now a little spooked whenever they stayed at my place, which I totally understood. I had the same fears too. Never again would I go to bed in that house with any window open, even a small crack. Even though I preferred to experience the cool fresh air in the evening, when I was ready to go to bed, that luxury would now be a thing of the past. However, I thought what we all needed was some time to feel secure again, and eventually, my house would feel like a safe place again.

The following summer, Debbie and I decided to go to Galena for a golf weekend while the kids were staying at their dad's. JT and Jenny were responsible for coming over to my place twice a day to let the two dogs outside from their enclosed area in the laundry room. Jerry's sister had given me her pet, a sweet Doberman Pincher named Rhonda, to help with my security issues. Poochie was now very old and this younger dog might help alert me if she heard anything unusual. Plus, just the look of a Doberman can be very intimidating. On this particular day it was

Jenny's turn to check on the dogs, so she rode her bike over to the house, but upon entering she encountered quite a mess. The kitchen window had been broken and there was quite a bit of blood spattered around the walls and the floor. Instead of running away, she looked around the house to make sure no one was still there, and then contacted her dad. He came over to my house, brought Jenny back to his place, and sent a message to the golf course that I needed to call home. I was extremely upset that my home had been invaded again, and I had no idea if it was the same perpetrator as the year before. At least no one in my family had been hurt, except the intruder, who must have cut himself substantially from the broken glass of the kitchen window.

After my return home, I vowed that the kids and I would never stay overnight in that place again. And we never did. I moved out and found a two-bedroom condominium on the third floor with underground parking. I felt that if someone were ever to follow me, I would disappear into a large building where it would be very difficult to know which precise apartment within the building belonged to me. Jen really liked the idea of living in this new type of home, especially since her best friend, Holly, lived in the same complex. There were no yards to mow, no snow to shovel, and there was a beautiful swimming pool to use in the summer. JT, however, now preferred spending more of his time at his dad's house, where there was less supervision over him than at my place. He was a young teenager and liked the newfound freedom he was experiencing at his dad's house.

Jerry and I had agreed to relax the precise routine outlined in our divorce decree to now allow more flexibility for the kid's location based on their schedules. Jenny continued to share her time fairly evenly between the two homes, even though her brother was staying with me less and less. I tried not to take JT's preference with his living arrangements as a personal affront to me, but understood that he was more comfortable in the environment at his dad's. What teenage boy would not like to be staying at a cool bachelor pad with little adult supervision? However, he learned that my job as a mother meant that I constantly needed to go over to his dad's to check up on him since my son did not always make the best decisions regarding his social life. I certainly did not catch all of JT's indiscretions, but I know that I managed to foil some of his attempts at providing a party atmosphere at his dad's house. Although Jenny was no angel, I didn't feel the need to constantly check on her behavior as she became more independent in high school. She was much less of a daredevil than JT, and her social group of friends seemed to be fairly trustworthy.

Even though I experienced a lot of worry and concern over the wellbeing of my children, I ended up surviving the trials and tribulations of raising two extremely socially-active teenagers! They both were physically healthy, emotionally well-adjusted, and were blessed with many good friends as well. I cannot take all the credit for raising two good kids, since their dad had a presence in their lives too. Both Jerry and I, although through separate means, laid the groundwork for two kids to grow, prosper, and become responsible young adults. My primary goal in life had been accomplished: my kids made it though high school alive and well!

Chapter 25

A New Chapter

With the arrival of a new decade, the 90s, I was ready for another change of residence. JT was now a sophomore in college attending Colorado State, and Jen would be beginning her education at the University of Colorado that upcoming fall. I was going to be on my own now, at least as far as a living arrangement was concerned. Although convenient and secure, condo living had become too restrictive for me. I missed having an attached garage and yearned for a little garden area. If I could find a place with upstairs bedrooms, I could enjoy having open-air ventilation in the evening too. So I found a roomy, three-bedroom townhouse that fit my criteria. The assessment fees were low even though there was a nice pool and small lake in the development. Being fairly tranquil, this area seemed to attract many retired folks, which I found appealing too. There were many eyes and ears constantly checking out the neighborhood for security concerns. This place just had a real homey feel to it.

My initial plan for remodeling this older townhouse was to have hardwood floors installed in the kitchen and to have the rest of the oak flooring refinished. A friend of mine recommended a local fireman, Dan, who did excellent work at a fair price. So, I proceeded to hire him and was pleased with his work. I knew that I would need his help in the future, since I had other remodeling plans in mind. We stayed in touch over the next year and eventually began to date when Dan found himself suddenly single. Both of us had kids the same ages: he had two beautiful daughters,

Katie and Dani, who both were also away at college. Dan and I had a plenty of free time to develop a nice relationship without the distractions of dealing with each other's children.

Since I had been single for thirteen years, I was looking forward to the possibility of entering into the marriage scene again. On my forty-third birthday, Dan asked me to marry him while we were dining out at a cute little Italian restaurant. I was happy that he finally got around to proposing and was anxious to plan a wedding. We both wanted it to be a small affair with only close family members attending the service. August 8, 1992 was picked for our wedding date because it was the only Saturday that all four kids would be available that summer. It was important to me that both sides of our families would be able to meet one another. All four kids stood up for us at the ceremony that was held in my townhouse. Then we celebrated our marriage for the remainder of the weekend with twenty-two family members in Lake Wisconsin where Dan and his sister, Karen, shared a cute summer cottage. After our celebratory weekend, the kids would be leaving home for each of their respective colleges, and Dan and I began living as husband and wife.

After a couple of years, JT, Jenny, Katie, and Dani were also looking for new directions in their lives: they all received college degrees and began seeking new roots for themselves. Dan and I lived in my townhouse, continued to do more remodeling, and were basically content with our daily routines. Dan was advancing up the ladder in the fire department, eventually earning the title of Deputy Chief, and I was continuing to accumulate more years of experience of teaching at Carl Sandburg. We had our eyes on early retirement options that were available to both of us in the following decade.

Dan had continued to do side jobs as a carpenter, which meant he built homes for everyone else, but never for himself. So in the summer of 2000, he bought a lot on South Turtle Lake in the Northwoods of Wisconsin with plans of building his own lake house. The heavily wooded lot was situated on a small bay within a three-chain lake system. We both loved this unspoiled area that had an abundance of wildlife, clear water, and beautiful forests of towering pines, majestic hemlocks, white birch, and sugar maples. Dan decided to retire at the end of the year from the fire department, so he would be young enough, at the age of fifty-five, to begin working on the carpentry involved with this new construction project.

The following summer, Dan was busy with the first stage of the project, the garage. Even though I loved spending much of that summer in the Northwoods, I needed to return to Illinois to begin another school year. Dan remained up north to do as much construction on the garage in the autumn as possible, before the weather turned cold and miserable. I had been back teaching that fall only for about three weeks, when some disconcerting news was spreading around the building. There was a report of an airplane that had crashed into one of the buildings in New York City. Initially, I did not think very much about the incident and assumed that a very small prop plane must have hit one of the buildings. However, it soon became apparent that this event was no minor accident. Terrorists had planned the suicide hijacking of four commercial jets and had flown two of these large planes into each of the Twin Towers of the World Trade Center. Both buildings collapsed killing almost three thousand people. The financial center of New York looked like an atomic bomb had hit the area with huge clouds of destruction roaring down the streets.

I was watching the news coverage on the library's television along with some other faculty members in total shock. I could not believe my eyes that this destruction was occurring in our country and no one could explain the reason for all this ruin. A third plane, which had been headed for our nation's capital, crashed in Pennsylvania killing all forty passengers on board. Some of the captive passengers had tried to gain control of the aircraft, but failed in their attempt and the plane crashed prematurely in a farmer's field. However, their heroism saved many lives of government personnel working in The White House that day. A forth plane crashed into one of the wings in the Pentagon incurring a death toll of 189. I thought about Dan working on his garage in the serene woods in Wisconsin and, even though most of the world was glued to the television coverage, he did not have a clue that such a tremendous change was occurring in our country. And I had no way of contacting him until later that evening when I discovered that he eventually had been made aware of the tragic turn of events from a friend who lived nearby.

This horrific day, September 11, 2001, was the most surreal day of my life. No one knew how many more hijacked planes could still be threatening us and how many more areas of the country could be affected. However, within several hours, most of the air traffic in our country was safely grounded. The country's normal activities were halted for the next couple of weeks and Americans would learn how much hatred of us had existed, particularly from people living in Islamic countries.

Our country now has entered a new era: one of aggressively fighting terrorism. These attacks were the first ones on American soil since the bombing of Pearl Harbor in 1941. This country would never be the same again. Prior to 9/11, most Americans were quite a bit naïve over the lack of respect the U. S. held throughout the rest of the world. One of the main sources of agitation from these religious groups was the fact that United States' troops had been treading on the holy lands in Saudi Arabia. This activity was totally unacceptable to some of the religious extremists. Camps were developed in Afghanistan to train young Moslem men to fight and carry out their crusade against Western civilization. Although the hijackers from September 11th were mostly from Saudi Arabia, they had trained in camps in Afghanistan. So it seemed reasonable for our country to wage a war against a region that was allowing these radical religious groups to learn combat techniques to perform acts of terror targeted at the United States. However, as I currently am writing this memoir, the conflict with Afghanistan has been the longest war that the U. S. has been engaged throughout the history of our country. The current Administration's goal is to help the Afghan people acquire a stable government so that the U.S. forces would be able to withdraw from the area. America's battle against terrorism will probably be an ongoing one for many, many years to come, but it may not necessarily be one of physical combat. Our country will continue to constantly be on the defensive to protect our land and our citizens.

Even though our country had been wounded with the events of September 11th, eventually life in America returned to a new normalcy. Travel by air meant more detailed security checks, but people gradually resumed the types of activities that were done before this major incident. My life also returned to normal doing the things that I enjoyed, especially traveling to see my kids. JT has remained in Colorado earning a living as a musician and fathered a son named Romey. He is married to a wonderful woman named Moira. Jenny has been working in the field of charitable giving, and has had the courage to battle a horrific disease, breast cancer. Jenny, who moved to San Francisco, has waged her battle against this disease in the most unselfish, determined manner. Her husband Ashley has been her advocate during her struggle with the disease. Katie became a nurse, married Jeff, and ended up in Kansas City with three children, Jack, Anna, and Sarah. And Dani was the only one to remain in Northwest suburbs, married Joe, and has two children, Joey and Maddie.

Dan would eventually finish constructing **a** beautiful home in northern Wisconsin. One of our goals was to have a place that the kids and grandkids could congregate while enjoying each other's company, as well as indulging in many healthy outdoor activities. We feel so very fortunate to be able to have such a place. In the summer, there's an abundance of activities for everyone: swimming, canoeing, kayaking, fishing, biking, and just plain hiking through the fields of wildflowers and thick forests. Our property in the fall is a beautiful mixture of colors ranging from the scarlet reds and oranges of the sugar maples scattered among different blends of greens of the hemlocks and pine trees. Even in the winter, there is a lot of potential to enjoy the outdoors; ice fishing, snow-fort building, cross-country and downhill skiing are all close by.

I was able to retire from my job as an educator in June 2006 after thirty-two years of teaching in the same school, Carl Sandburg, where I had made so many of my closest friends. Jan, Nancy, Mary, Allen, Burgy, and Julie are a few of the people who I would like to thank for helping me through some of my toughest times as well as celebrating my most joyful ones. I'm also so very proud of JT and Jenny who in adulthood have become strong, compassionate, loving individuals. As part of my retirement gift to myself, I became the mother of another little girl, a black lab mixed-breed puppy named Jellybean, who was rescued from a kill shelter. She has provided Dan and me with more love, dedication, and enjoyment than we could have ever imagined earlier in our marriage. Overall, I have been very blessed to have experienced the life that I have had. I certainly was able to learn from my mistakes, work hard for what was important to me, and appreciate all the good things that have come my way.

Chapter 26

November 4, 2008

What an exciting day for our country! I decided to journal my thoughts on this very special day. The emotional, hotly pursued race for President of the United States will be determined later today. Record numbers of Americans have been voting. There have been several "firsts" involved with this election between Republican nominee John McCain and Democratic nominee Barack Obama. Seventy-two year old McCain had picked a forty-four year old woman, Sarah Palin, for his running mate. If McCain would win, he would be the oldest elected President and have the first woman to be next in-line for the most powerful job in the world. Barack Obama, on the other hand, could become the first African American to assume the office of President if he amasses more electoral votes. Young people have been registering to vote all over the country and the early projections seem to favor Obama. The whole world would eagerly await the outcome of the election which would be announced after most of the polls close this evening. I'm so hopeful that we will have a change from the last eight years of Republican leadership.

In 2000, George W. Bush had won the election by a narrow margin. Actually, the Supreme Court had to decide the outcome of the election due to problems with voting irregularities in Florida. Democrat Al Gore had won the popular vote, but narrowly lost the electoral votes. Within nine months of Bush's inauguration, the September 11th attacks occurred. Democrats, Republicans, and the whole country were firmly behind the initial plans that Bush had set in motion to retaliate against the Afghan training camps.

However, the Republican administration used scare tactics to convince the American people that we also needed to invade another Moslem country, Iraq, which had nothing to do with the 9/11 attacks. So we entered a second war needlessly because the American people had placed their trust in the Republican leadership. At this time, Barack Obama, a state senator from Illinois, vigorously denounced the Bush policies of pursuing a war in Iraq. Most Americans now agree that Obama's judgment turned out to be correct: we should have never entered that war. The whole situation reminded me of the Vietnam War, which was very unpopular in the late 60s and early 70s. Both wars had divided the people of our country and, in my opinion, led to unnecessary deaths of United States soldiers.

When Bush won re-election in 2004, I was shocked! One of the big debates in this election was whether homosexuals could enter into legal marriages. This unjust war was a huge issue, but the Republican strategists were able to divert the attention to the war with homophobic concerns during the campaign. Bush was therefore given another four years to lead our country. By the end of his term, however, his approval ratings were dismal and people wanted a change in leadership. The economy had been nose-diving during Bush's administration; some people had been calling it a depression. The economic downturn was probably the most compelling reason that the undecided voters, at the last minute, leaned toward the Democratic Party. Bush may not have been entirely responsible for the economic mess, but the American people were angry and wanted to send a message to Washington.

2008 was the right time for the American people to show that the policies from the Bush administration were no longer going to be tolerated. By eight o'clock in the evening, the television news reporters were predicting a win for Obama. Shortly thereafter, McCain gave a gracious concession speech in which he encouraged American citizens to throw their support behind his rival, Barack Obama. At eleven o'clock, Barack was addressing the crowd in Grant Park in downtown Chicago. I did not attend it personally, but enjoyed watching this momentous speech on television in my home. It was another great speech from Obama and an unforgettable day for me to see an African American overcome the race issue and become our next qualified leader. Most people at the rally, whether they were black, white, or whatever, were shown with tears streaming down their cheeks feeling honored to be able to witness such a social change: the fact that a black man could become President of the United States! It's going to be a rough road for Barack Obama especially with the economy on the verge of collapse, but it seems as though he has the intelligence and vision to get our country back on the right path. I'm as proud as ever of our country and am hopeful that Barack Obama will make some major changes for future generations. I hope my grandkids reap the benefits! Only time will only tell.

Chapter 27

We've Come a Long Way Baby!

Besides the issues of race affecting people in our country, the gender gap has greatly narrowed as I complete this memoir. Reflecting on the fact that both of my grandmothers were not given the right to vote until they reached middle age, I appreciate how far this country has come to give women equal rights. Although extremely controversial the 1973 Rowe v. Wade decision gave women the right to have a choice over the difficult, heart-wrenching decision of whether to terminate a pregnancy. The passage of Title IX insured that equal opportunities exist in sports for young women. Sally Ride, who is two years younger than I, became the first woman to travel in space in 1984. When a person qualifies to obtain a mortgage for a home today, it is not determined by someone's gender, but instead on a person's financial history. In fact, currently it's fairly common for the woman in the household to be the one that qualifies for a loan. In fact more women, than men are finishing college with bachelor degrees, and equal numbers of men and women are pursuing advanced degrees in medicine and law. If I were to ask one of my grandchildren to close his or her eyes and imagine what a typical medical doctor might look like, I doubt if he or she would have visualized a Caucasian male (but I'm sure the white lab coat would still be there!) More women than ever are becoming judges, politicians, and other high-ranking government officials. A woman can now join the military if she so desires and can honorably serve our country. Often it is the father instead of the mother who stays home to care for the children; a married couple can decide what arrangement works best for them. A single or gay woman can become a mother through invitro-fertilization or adoption; society is learning to accept different structures of family life. A mother can choose to work outside the home without tremendous guilt, but can also feel productive in the role as homemaker. President Obama, as one of his first legislative measures in office, signed the Lilly Ledbettor Law which gives women the legal right of receiving equal pay for doing equal work. Women certainly have come such a long way now that we have entered the 21st century and made big strides towards equality.

When I was growing up, my parents and teachers gave me the message that all fields of endeavor were possible for a woman, and, through education, my goals could be achieved. It has taken most of my lifetime to witness so many advances in equal rights, and we have only just begun! One of my favorite quotes is from an African proverb via Greg Mortensen and his book, *Three Cups of Tea: One Man's Mission to Promote Peace...One school at a Time:* "Educate a boy, and you educate an individual. Educate a girl, and you educate a community." Hopefully, as women become even more influential, the world will continue to improve.

XXXXXXXXXXXXXXXXXXXXXXXXXXXXXXXXXX

I sincerely hope that sharing my thoughts and experiences may provide an understanding of a very interesting time in which to live witnessing the most recent chapters in American history. Even though there have been so many transitions in our society during my lifetime, some things will never change. Growing up is a difficult process, no matter what generation in which a person is born. And our deep, emotional connections to one another will continue to exemplify the true meaning of life. I only wish I would have had the opportunity to read what my parents, grandparents, and great-grandparents thought during so many of their struggles and joys that they had encountered during their lives!

Photo Gallery

Mom
Elizabeth Williams

Dad Graduation Picture
Vernon Frank Trost

Grandma Trost

Edna, Elmer, and Norbert Trost, 1915
Dad's Siblings

Dad, last row, dark sweater

Dad

Mom

Little Sis, Mom with Ella

Dorothy and Mom, 1941

Sisters, Ella and Mom

Mom and Dad wed, Aug. 4 1945

Uncle George during WWII

Mom's brother, George, with his wife, Helen

Mom's brother, Jim, with his wife, Doris

Mom's brother, John, with his wife, Lil

Grandma, Mom, Vernon, Dad

Vernon and Joyce, 1950

Joyce and Vernon, 1954

Joyce, Vernon, and Cheryl, 1960

Dad and Mom at the beach

Vacation Ride

8th grade cheerleader

Baby Cheryl and Joyce

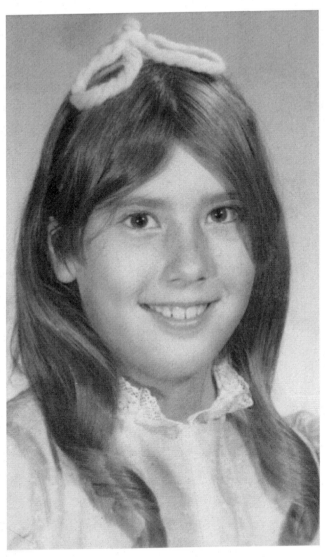

Cheryl's school picture

Joyce with Carolyn, 8ᵗʰ grade graduation

Pom-pon girl

JT's baby picture

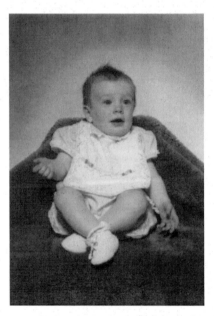

Jenny's baby picture

2nd year of teaching

Carl Sandburg Science Dept. '76

Joyce, Jenny, JT, 1987

JT, Joyce, Dan, Jen, Aug. 8, 1992

Dani, Dan, Joyce, Katie, Aug. 8, 1992